EACH BELONGS

The Remarkable Story of the First School System to Move to Inclusion

Jim Hansen

with

Gerv Leyden • Gary Bunch • Jack Pearpoint

Library and Archives Canada Cataloguing in Publication

Hansen, Jim
Each Belongs, the story of the first inclusive school board/Jim Hansen;
with Gerv Leyden, Gary Bunch and Jack Pearpoint

Includes bibliographical references.

ISBN 1-895418-58-5

1. Each Belongs. I. Hansen, Jim   II. Title

HV8688.L63 2006   364.6'8   C2005-901061-4

First Edition - 2006

Printing: Couto Printing, Toronto, Canada. 2006

Cover photo:
Jim Hansen welcoming Rose Galati and her late daughter Maria at the Summer
Institute. A young friend and Marsha Forest look on in the background.
(photo - Jack Pearpoint)

INCLUSION PRESS
24 Thome Crescent, Toronto, Ontario Canada M6H 2S5
TEL: (416) 658-5363 FAX: (416) 658-5067
E-mail: inclusionpress@inclusion.com
Web Page: www.inclusion.com

Each Belongs Credo

- Each person is endowed with the dignity of a person.

- Each person has equal value despite differences in ability.

- Each person has a right to grow and indeed each person can grow.

- The limits of individual growth are unknown and should
  not be circumscribed.

- No person is static, each is ever in the process of becoming.

- Each person is unique and irrepeatable.

- The beliefs we hold about people can serve as prison walls
  limiting us at every turn.

- They can also set us free from our shackles to confront
  great new possibilities never dreamed of before.

- Life is the ultimate gift and learning is its crowning.

Table of Contents

MARSHA FOREST (1942-2000) INSPIRED OTHERS WITH HER PASSIONATE AND UNCOMPROMISING ADVOCACY FOR INCLUSION. **A MARSHA FOREST BOOK** COMMUNICATES IN HER SPIRIT.

Preface

This book is the untold story of the history of inclusion in Ontario. To the best of our knowledge, although there were spotty examples of excellence in 'Inclusion" throughout Canada, United States and UK, the Hamilton-Wentworth Catholic District School Board (HWCDSB) was the first school system anywhere to welcome ALL students into a fully inclusive system.

This book is important because this story, this amazing history remains unknown – often virtually denied. We see Each Belongs as a tool for families, advocates, teachers, principals, school board members and policy makers. They can hold it up and say, "It can be done", and "If they have been doing it for over 30 years, we can do it here."

This book is a revision of Jim Hansen's original **Each Belongs**, the story of the change of the Hamilton-Wentworth Catholic District School Board from the segregated special education model to a fully inclusive system for students with disabilities. When it was suggested that the HWCDSB story would benefit from editing and from the addition of information on the status of inclusive education in the world today, our editorial team undertook the task. To the best of our ability we have retained Jim's voice in telling the story. It is only in this preface, the introductory chapter, and the closing chapter, that our voices are heard. Otherwise, to the degree possible in a revised version of the text, it is Jim's voice that you hear. It is the voice you should hear.

We write this revised version of Jim's **Each Belongs** some years after he and his colleagues pioneered inclusive education in the Hamilton-Wentworth Catholic District School Board (HWCDSB) beginning in the late 1960's and early 1970's. This difference in time between then and now calls for a number of explanations of the context in which reform to inclusion occurred in HWCDSB, and the context in which we write about it today.

It was not until 1989 that the term inclusive education was coined in Toronto, Ontario. To that point, integration was the term favoured for description of placement of students with disabilities in regular classrooms. It is a term used today by many. However, integration

I like it here because the people treat me normal and its fun. But we need more ramps to get into the lunchroom and a elevator to go upstairs.

Joe, Grade 3

We are all humans, we all have the right to live and learn and grow.

Liz

A note about the photos

The photos throughout the book are a selection from slide shows made by the Hamilton-Wentworth Catholic District School Board for public presentations. Most are older - reflecting the early origins of full inclusion in the Board.

Other photos are by Jack Pearpoint

is associated with special education. In turn, special education reflects belief that some students with disabilities must be segregated for their learning, and that those "integrated" at any time may have their placement changed to a fully or partially segregated placement, if found necessary. In some instances, integration is used to refer to classes of students with special needs who spend no time at all in regular classes with typical students. The catalyst for placement under special education, that which necessitates change, is whether the academic or social level of any student is acceptably similar to those of students without disabilities. If they are seen as similar, the student remains integrated in the regular classroom. If either academic or social strength is found wanting, a decision is made whether to transfer the student to a more specialized setting.

Inclusion, in comparison, does not change the placement of any student. All students begin in and remain in regular classrooms. Inclusion makes changes in regular classrooms to accommodate students' academic and social abilities. When the term integration is used in conjunction with HWCDSB and its change to inclusion in the period of Jim Hansen's narrative, it is not used in the special education sense, but in the contemporary inclusion sense. All students, disabled or not, are placed full-time in regular classrooms, and are supported there.

Other terminology has changed as well. For instance, there are references to students identified as being 'trainable retarded" in Jim's narrative. This is a term no longer used to describe students with intellectual challenge in HWCDSB or, indeed, throughout the province of Ontario. Terms such as developmental delay or intellectual challenge or slow learner are the norm. Though opposed in general to the use of labels to identify students in daily education, HWCDSB does use those required by the Ministry of Education when necessary.

Jim's original **Each Belongs** had a large closing section devoted to letters and notes from fellow-workers, parents, and others commenting on the experience of reforming education, not only for students with disabilities, but for all students in HWCDSB. For editorial reasons it was decided that this revision would not dedicate as much space to these communications as had the original **Each Belongs**. However, the sense of what people had to say about

These exceptional students belong in our school. They are quite nice to be with and can turn a dull day into an exciting one. They should not be separated from us. That would be like discrimination.

Rosalba, Grade 8

A note about quotations

The majority of the quotations used to illustrate the text are from children, parents, teachers, principals, Board staff and others associated with the development of 'Each Belongs' from its earliest years or more recently. We have made it quite clear when using other sources.

the pioneering move of HWCDSB had to be retained. We, therefore, have retained the voices of these commentators as a running accompaniment to Jim's narrative. These commentators played an integral part in the amazing move to inclusion made in HWCDSB. We hope we have not diminished their role and contribution in any way.

It would be remiss of us if we were not to mention the myriad of visitors who journeyed to Hamilton to see the HWCDSB inclusion program in action. They came from every part of the globe, and continue to do so. Some came so that they could leave and declare inclusion a myth, a wonderful concept but impossible to implement. These did not carry away any message of new ways to understand, respect, and work with learners with disabilities in education. Others came to learn. They left with new ideas of what might be. Some worked to move their local education systems toward the future. Visitors from across the globe continue to visit the HWCDSB.

Finally, Jim, his colleagues, and we, have no intent of claiming that HWCDSB invented inclusion or led the world to inclusion. There were glimmerings of inclusive thought and practice in many places during the 1960's and 1970's. The particular value of this book is that it records the move from segregated special education to inclusion of an entire school system, the first, we believe, to make such a move.

Gerv Leyden

Gary Bunch

Jack Pearpoint

2006

Inclusive Education:
Leadership, Change, and Today's Context

This book is about vision and leadership toward a revolutionary new form of education for learners with disabilities. The leadership took place in a modest-sized Canadian school system where, Jim Hansen, a determined leader, and his colleagues had a radical new vision of what education for students with disabilities might be. That system was the Hamilton-Wentworth Catholic District School Board (HWCDSB), formerly the Hamilton-Wentworth Separate School Board. Those around Jim, his fellow administrators, classroom teachers, special education teachers, and parents of all students in HWCDSB, had the courage and trust to risk a pioneering journey toward inclusive education. It seemed to them that differences in ability to read and write, or to behave well at all times, were poor reasons to separate learners from their friends in the regular school community. Hamilton-Wentworth moved away from an educational belief which segregated learners with disabilities in special classrooms and special schools, and took the path to inclusion where all students, abled and disabled, study and learn together in the regular classrooms of the school down the street.

In doing so, the Board brought more than education to learners with disabilities and to the entire HWCDSB system. It brought human rights and social justice. That journey to social justice, however, is not the focus of this first chapter. That story will be told by Jim and his colleagues in following chapters. This chapter is about all those others across the globe who have realized the inherent unfairness and social injustice of segregated education: all those who have joined the HWCDSB journey over the years, and why more and more are creating their own path to that goal. The revolution toward inclusive education for all learners now stretches over every continent. This opening chapter tries to give a sense of this global change, and the vision that impels it.

In the past, society viewed persons who happen to have a disability as having special educational needs. This concept of special needs led to the erroneous belief that persons with disabilities were incompetent and required extraordinary support. They were so different in their learning that they could not be expected to learn alongside typical learners, and typical learners were affected negatively by their presence. Though inclusion now has disproved

What seems common to all the schools we have visited is strong leadership and a 'can do' attitude. What the schools demonstrate is a willingness to enrol disabled pupils as a matter of course and as part of the local community and then to make the adjustments that are necessary for them to participate, as fully as possible.

Reasonable Adjustments Project
(United Kingdom)

Some data are available which reveal trends over time. In general terms countries are increasingly moving to inclusive provision.

(Organization of Cooperation & Development)

these beliefs, they led to creation of two parallel education systems; the regular system for typical learners and the system of labelling, special schools, special classes, special teachers, special buses, and special curricula for learners with disabilities. Many governments and educators have chosen not to move from, and continued to follow, the special education approach. The fact that placement in segregated educational settings carried with it reduction of personal autonomy and an impoverished social life was, and is, considered a necessary loss justified by the need for special education. The fact that research documents the advantages of inclusion is considered irrelevant. To these people, inclusive education is a pipe-dream. This is one way of thinking about education and persons with disabilities. It is the way most educators across the world were thinking in the late 1960's, and the way too many continue to think today.

Thinking Differently

It is not the way that Jim Hansen and his colleagues in Hamilton-Wentworth were thinking. They were thinking about how to bring children together in learning, not how to separate them. Society is struggling toward the "rights" perspective in education. In essence, this perspective says that a person with disabilities has the same rights as anyone else. It says that, "Yes. A person with disabilities is different in some ways from the majority of community members. Yes. A learner with disabilities may need educational supports to learn effectively in a regular classroom". But the rights perspective also says, "No! Difference in ability does not mean that the person loses rights to live and participate fully in society. Just as we do not separate learners on the basis of gender, race, culture, or ethnicity, we should not separate them on the basis of difference in ability".

I want to show people that we should be friends with everyone.

Michael, Grade 12

This fact has been emphasized most strongly by the United Nations. In 1989, the United Nations Convention on the Rights of the Child set out children's rights in respect to freedom from discrimination, and in respect to the representation of their wishes and views. The Convention was followed in 1994 by the United Nations Educational, Scientific, and Cultural Organization (UNESCO) Salamanca Statement. The Salamanca Statement called all governments to move to inclusive education as the strongest and most equitable way to address educational needs of all learners. Many nations now have subscribed to the Salamanca Statement and are moving in different ways to implement its spirit. It is worthwhile to provide some of the essential points of the Salamanca Statement, and to indicate what results are to flow from it.

UNESCO's Salamanca Statement says that:
- Every child has a basic right to education
- Every child has unique characteristics, interests, abilities, and learning needs
- Educational services should take into account these diverse characteristics and needs
- Those with special educational needs must have access to regular schools
- Regular schools with an inclusive ethos are the most effective way to combat discriminatory attitudes, create welcoming and inclusive communities, and achieve education for all
- Such schools provide effective education to the majority of children, improve efficiency and cost-effectiveness

The right to education for people with disabilities as well as inclusive education should be included in the countries' National Plan for Education.
(UNESCO & the University of Oslo)

The Salamanca Statement asks governments to take steps to:
- Give the highest priority to making education systems inclusive
- Adopt the principle of inclusive education as a matter of law or policy
- Develop demonstration projects
- Set up ways to plan, monitor, and evaluate educational provision for children and adults
- Encourage and make easy the participation of parents and organizations of disabled people
- Invest in vocational aspects of inclusive education
- Make sure there are adequate teacher education programs

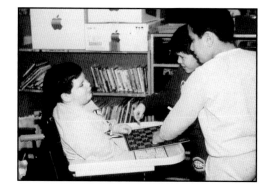

In a 1999 review of progress toward inclusion, UNESCO affirmed that inclusion is an essential part of ensuring that students with disabilities have equal access to community schools and equal learning opportunities.

Inclusion is to be seen as part of the wider struggle to overcome exclusive discourse and practices, and against the ideology that each individual is completely separate and independent. Inclusion is about the improvement of schooling. Rather than being a marginal theme concerned how a relatively small group of pupils might be attached to mainstream schools, it lays the foundations for an approach that could lead to the transformation of the system itself.

Hamilton-Wentworth Catholic District School Board accomplished, beginning in the 1960's and 1970's, what the United Nations and UNESCO asked in the 1980's and 1990's. They did it before the term "inclusion" was coined in Toronto, Canada in the late 1980's. They did it while others were talking about doing it. As far as we know, it was the first full school system anywhere to begin the journey to inclusive education.

Today HWCDSB has approximately 30,000 students. It does not have a single special class. It does not have a single special school. All students attend regular classrooms in community schools alongside their typical peers. Regular classroom teachers, supported by administrators and special education teachers, welcome and teach all students. Learning for all students, regardless of any type of difference, is alive and well for all students in the HWCDSB system.

Change at the Canadian Level

In the 1980's and 1990's international leadership began to catch up with this small Canadian school system. Today, various governments are acting to recognize the right of learners with disabilities to a community-based inclusive education in the company of their typical peers. Some governments, particularly those which are income-rich, simply have emphasized the integration component of the special education model; students with disabilities may be permitted to attend regular classrooms, if they are not perceived as "too different" and as long as they keep up an unspecified pace of achievement. Such governments retain the full, increasingly segregated, spectrum of the special education model for those who are too different or who find need for a "too" individual pace of learning. Other governments, both in income-rich and income-poor nations, have declared for inclusion and are working at implementing it in place of their former special education models.

Inclusive Jurisdictions – Canada
- *New Brunswick*
- *Yukon*
- *Northwest Territory*
- *Nunavut*

I like it here because the people treat me normal and its fun. But we need more ramps to get into the lunchroom and elevator to go upstairs.

Joe, Grade 3

In this account we are focusing on inclusive leadership in a single school system in Hamilton. What is happening elsewhere in Canada? Definite movement toward inclusion is apparent, though most provincial governments and educators resist change from the special education model. They have the evidence that inclusion works and that inclusion is inherently fair. However, their political will is not strong enough for them to face the stresses of change. Exceptions are the province of New Brunswick and the territories of Yukon, Northwest Territories, and Nunavut, all of which have declared policies of inclusion. In other parts of the land, individual school systems and individual schools have declared for inclusion. More and more Canadian governments and educators are listening to parents and people with disabilities who advocate for inclusion. We forecast that, despite hesitation in parts of Canada, movement to inclusion will continue as evidence and advocacy mount.

Beyond the formal Canadian education system, a number of agencies advocate inclusion in education. Examples of these are the Canadian Association for Community Living, a national association working with and for Canadians with intellectual challenge, and the Ontario Coalition for Inclusive Education, a provincial group representing organizations such as the Down Syndrome Association and Family Alliance. The federal government has a strengthening record of supporting research and resource development. The Marsha Forest Centre, the primary mover for this book, is an inclusive agency whose modest size belies its effects. The Centre is the well-spring of such internationally known strategies as Circle of Friends, MAPS, PATH, and, more recently, the school-based national advocacy system for disability and education, PlayFair Teams. Closely allied to the Centre, and supporting its publishing activities, is Inclusion Press, Canada's only press devoted to disability, advocacy, and social justice. Such infrastructures will support continued movement to inclusion.

All my life, I was judged, put down and left out of things just because I am physically disabled, but for once I'm not. I guess it's true. People have no idea how powerful they are.

Megan

Change at the International Level

What has been happening beyond Canada? In some nations, inclusive education has become a major dynamic in educational reform. An increasing number of schools have changed direction. Legislation has been passed. Teacher preparation has been affected. Resources have been developed. In other nations recognition, acceptance, and change have been less swift and pervasive. However, it is safe to say that in a surprising number of countries, inclusive education is on the educator agenda, on the parents' agenda, on the persons' with disabilities agenda, and on the government's agenda. It seems that evidence of inclusive education may be found wherever one goes.

The following are brief looks at a number of nations from all parts of the globe. We offer them to give you a sense of how far and wide the educational revolution first seen at the school system level in Hamilton, Ontario has spread.

✔ **Italy** has been considered by many to be the most inclusive nation in the world. Government policy, since the 1970's, has emphasized inclusive education. Legislation abolishing special classes for learners of statutory school age was passed in 1977. Students formerly placed in special classes are now included in general education. A number of other supporting pieces of legislation have been passed since 1977.

✔ Across the Adriatic Sea from Italy in Southeast Europe are the nations of the **former Yugoslavia**. In each of these nations, interest in inclusive education is rising up the agenda. Persons with disabilities, parents, advocates, and some educators and government officials are lobbying for change toward inclusive education. Faculty in some universities (e.g. Zagreb, Tuzla) offer instruction in inclusive education to future teachers. However, movement from the highly segregation-based Soviet model of education and recent war has held change back. Nevertheless, inclusion is being discussed and advocated with increasing vigour in the war-torn nations of Southeast Europe.

At the Marsha Forest Centre, we can attest to this fact personally. Two of us attended an inclusive education project meeting in Slovenia last year. Representatives of almost all the nations of Southeast Europe were there. We were discussing the possibility of a joint inclusive education initiative in the region.

✔ **Malta** is a tiny nation known for the friendliness and courage of its people. It also is one of the smallest nations in terms of size and population. Politically, Malta has two parties. Both support inclusive education. Determined efforts have resulted in positive legislation, development of a new and inclusive curriculum, and development of programs at the University of Malta to prepare teachers and classroom support staff. The 8th principle of the new national curriculum is:

In some countries, such as Italy, there has been a long preoccupation with this issue with inclusive education becoming the norm and readily accepted by teachers and pupils alike.
(Students with Disabilities in Mainstream Schools, OECD)

Inclusive education cannot be seen as a specific issue, but must be regarded as an approach to the development of the entire school system.
Nynke Dijkstra & Willemein Vrielink (Netherlands)   (Romania)

An inclusive education is based on a commitment on the part of the learning community, to fully acknowledge individual difference and to professing as well as implementing inclusionary politics.
National Minimum Curriculum (Malta)

An inclusive education is based on a commitment, on the part of the learning community, to fully acknowledge individual difference and to professing as well as implementing inclusionary politics. This concept recognizes the full range of educational interests, potential and needs of students.

Representatives of the Marsha Forest Centre have had the pleasure of visiting Malta for discussions on inclusive education with local advocates, faculty of the university, and a Member of Parliament. We also had the additional pleasure of arranging a visit to the Hamilton-Wentworth Catholic Board for one of the leading inclusive educators of Malta. We continue to work together.

✔ **South Africa** continues to emerge from a past where difference mattered, and mattered very much. However, positive moves have been made in disability and education in South Africa. One of the dynamics is embodied in the recent White Paper 6 on Special Needs Education: Building an Inclusive Education and Training System. Inclusive education is defined as a learning environment that promotes the full personal, academic and professional development of all learners irrespective of race, class, gender, disability, religion, culture, sexual preference, learning styles, and language. Within this general definition, it is recognized that the inclusion of learners with "special education needs" or "learning barriers" in mainstream classes, is part of a universal human rights movement. South Africa is in the first two years of a 20 year implementation period for inclusive education.

✔ The following email is but one example of the communications being received at the MFC from from across the world.

Hello all.
My name is V. R.. I am special teacher from Russia. I am looking for information about inclusive education program. Where do I get titles, and possibly texts, of research papers comparing outcomes of inclusive and special environments for special needs children? Preferably recent and authoritative. What would be, broadly, the structure of a university teacher-training course in inclusive education?

The conviction that "inclusion" is, at root, a matter of equality of rights and opportunities is understood by many who advocate for a fair and just education system.
John Kenworthy & Joe Whittaker (England)

✔   **China**, the most populous nation in the world, is often considered slow to change and with a decidedly traditional education system. Friends from China, the international litera-ture, and a recent Hong Kong conference on inclusive education, suggest growing activity around disability and education. There is evidence that the government is beginning to sup-port a movement to educate learners with disabilities in regular classrooms. Though the term inclusive education is not used in China, the term 'disabled children learning in regular classes", as used by a Chinese researcher at a recent conference in Warsaw, appears to be a synonym. In addition, government political statements have indicated that China's population of persons with disabilities is so great, that it is not financially feasible to meet their needs through de-velopment of segregated special education facilities. The solution to meeting needs in China, as well as other developing nations, seems to be to focus on the regular education system and inclusion.

✔   **Mongolia**, between China and Russia, is not a nation often thought of at meetings where inclusive education is discussed. However, inclusive education is a hot topic in Mongolia itself. Following dramatic political change in 1989 and subsequent collapse of the special school and residential care network for persons with disabilities, learners with disabilities be-came more visible as suffering from educational neglect and unproductive education. 1994 saw the introduction of integration programming supported by Save the Children, UK. Suc-cess of this program in 3 provinces and the capital city led to further work. By 2000 the Association of Parents with Disabled Children was a formally constituted NGO. In 2003, at an international workshop in Ulaanbaatar, the term inclusive education replaced the term integrated education.

This social revolution within our customs and traditions stems from our belief in inclusive education as the right of every handicapped child and the duty of our society.

(Mali)

✔   **Kenya** is another nation where inclusive education has appeared. With support from Leonard Cheshire International, an inclusive education program was initiated in Western Ke-nya in 2001. A core strategy has been development of inclusive learning environments with strong community involvement. Teacher education has begun, as has development of resource materials.

The continuing systemic changes in Israel regarding school inclusion and resource decentralization accentuate the importance of appropriate models in teacher training, and skill development, and setting design.

Michal Al-Yagon & Malka Margalit (Israel)

✔   **Nepal** has launched a serious effort to introduce inclusive education. Close connections to inclusive educators from the UK have been forged, as well as professional relationships with inclusive educators in India. One of our editorial team had opportunity to discuss inclusive education in Nepal with two officials of Nepal's Ministry of Education and Sports, Special Education section during a visit to Mumbai, India. Eight experienced school administrators and other Nepalese were graduating from an inclusive education training program at the National Resource Centre for Inclusive Education in Mumbai. Nepal exemplifies strong commitment to inclusive education.

✔   Here are excerpts from a freshly received e-mail from an educational official of the **Ivory Coast**. It was a request for the assistance of the Marsha Forest Centre. They sent us some details of their present plans for a five year program of conversion to inclusion.

I am responsible for the promotion of the population with disabilities in Ivory Coast. I must find a way for doing an inclusive education program for the 25,655 children with disabilities. Of this population, only 540 have access to special education. In accordance with the Salamanca conference, our Minister wants to achieve an inclusive education program in order to enable the children with disabilities to attend school like other children. The government agrees with the program. But it cannot do it alone.

Over the three years since its inception, Ugam has provided pre-school education for over 1200 children, irrespective of gender, religion, disability, caste, and socio-economic status, and created a cost effective model of inclusion in the community.

Mithu Alur (India)

✔   **India**, second most populous nation in the world, also is a nation with a formal policy of inclusion and recent evidence of implementation of the policy. For instance, all government schools recently have been directed to accept students with disabilities and include them in regular instruction. The Spastic Society of India is working toward inclusive education. In Mumbai the Society has established an extensive network of inclusive schools throughout the city. Originally developed by parents and their supporters as special schools, these are now moving to inclusion. One of the most exciting inclusive education programs we have seen is an early childhood program in the Dharavi slum, home to approximately 600,000 people. There, impoverished children from the slum, girl children, and children with disabilities are provided daily instruction based on an accepted early childhood education curriculum. Instruction in personal hygiene, nutrition, and English round out one of the world's most exciting early childhood programs.

The change is led from the Spastic Society school in Mumbai with strong support from Canadian inclusive educators and activists, as well as from the Canadian government. In 2004 an inclusive education project was initiated in Delhi by local authorities. This was not the first project in Delhi, but is the largest in that city. Some 100 schools are involved. The first step is familiarization of the administrators with inclusive philosophy, principles, and leadership. This is being accomplished with the assistance of faculty members of the University of Delhi.

These brief vignettes of activity around inclusive education provide an overview of activities in inclusive education from its first glimmerings in Hamilton, Canada to its rapid spread across the globe. We could add information on many other nations. Truly, inclusive education is an educational reform for which many in the world have been waiting. Activity level ranges from individual advocates to decisions by national governments. The most important thing to notice is that there is activity across the globe. Each nation will forge its own story of its own move to a new and socially just model for education and disability.

The Hamilton-Wentworth Catholic District School Board has made its move from special education to inclusion. This is its story. We hope you find it as inspiring as we have.

Pipe-dream, eh?

Read on and enjoy.

the editors

The group is mixed up with all kinds of colours and there is no-one who has to be integrated from outside because all are already inside – as people living in the neighbourhood they belong to and are welcomed in the school.
Andreas Hinz **(Germany)**

The Guitar
Barbara Italianio

People have been discussing the pros and cons of integration for many years. I believe that some, despite their efforts, are still no closer to the true meaning of inclusion.

Inclusion can not be written in a policy, yet it can be stated in a philosophy. However, even a policy cannot make people believe it, feel it, or live it. Our problem is that we try too hard to make an "inclusion program" work, rather than viewing inclusion as a natural way of life.

Today my son brought home a guitar he made in his woodworking class. It is the most beautiful, well-crafted instrument I have ever seen. I, like any parent, am proud to behold the talents and accomplishments of my children. This would be a very normal reaction for any parent, except that my child is blind, has cerebral palsy, and is intellectually challenged.

If all these things are true, my son's participation in the making of this musical instrument is very limited, then why is this guitar so special to me?

This guitar represents the true meaning of inclusion. The Hamilton-Wentworth Roman Catholic Separate School Board (H.W.R.C.S.S.B.) believes in the philosophy that each belongs and are working for a truly inclusive community. Once again these are only words unless they are being lived every moment of the day.

Last semester my son was enrolled in a woodworking class. His teacher never had special needs students in his class before. He was a little apprehensive at first, but expressed how he was willing to give it his best shot. He also stated that he would try and make this woodworking class as meaningful as possible for my son. He achieved this by finding out his interests. He discovered his love for music, and that his brother played the guitar. He then decided that by making a guitar he would be able to relate to what he was doing and the finished product could be shared with his brother and other people.

Throughout the semester, under the direction of the teacher, educational assistant, and his peers, a piece of wood was transformed and shaped into a beautiful musical instrument. At the same time my son's life has continued to grow by being part of the environment that told him he was valued and that he belonged. His peers were shown that being different doesn't mean being excluded. The school community benefitted because they couldn't help but be part of the positive feedback that was being conveyed throughout the school. They also knew that they had a direct part in the growth and development of my son.

Inclusion is probably one of our cheapest commodities. This is because it can't be bought. It is felt, it is lived, and it comes from the heart. It is based on the philosophy that each person is valued and has a right to live and be an active participant in their community no matter how great or small the contribution is. Each may belong, but this can only work if we let it.

The guitar is being placed on a stand in a prominent place in our home. It can be picked up and played at anytime, but it will always stand for a true symbol of inclusion and self-worth.

I would like to thank all the teachers and friends my son has had over the years in the school system. All these people had a direct part in building this guitar by giving of themselves and letting my son be and grow into the person he is today.

All students are special. If you can learn to make a guitar with the children who are designated "Special Needs", you have the ability to give the sense of value, dignity, and a presence of belonging to every student. You will have contributed to our community's future generation of people who will say that you may be limited in your ability to perform, but not in your ability to contribute.

Once again, I would like to thank the entire H.W.R.C.S.S.B. community for helping my son make his guitar.

Chapter 2
"Setting the Scene"

Mid 20th Century

It was exciting to be an educator in the late nineteen sixties and early seventies. Education was high on the list of government priorities. Money was therefore, relatively plentiful. The baby boom and immigration continued to swell the ranks of school attenders.

An accelerated housing programme created a demand for new schools and additions. Teachers were in great demand, but in short supply. New subdivisions and neighbourhoods seemed to spring up over night. In many places schools became the centre of the new community. Parents wanted and were encouraged to be part of their children's school and education.

The school setting and school life of my beginning years as a teacher were clearly about to change. It would prove to be a radical change and in my view a change for the better.

The stirring of the status quo created the climate for the tremendous achievements we've had in extending service to all our children, and particularly to those children with disabilities.

P.J. Brennan,
Emeritus Director of Education

First teaching class

My first teaching assignment was in St. Helen's, Toronto, 1952. I taught grades five and six, boys only. The thirty-four pupils in the room were mostly second generation English speaking Canadians. The curriculum was relatively simple and uniform throughout the province. It could be said, with only slight exaggeration, that through any open classroom window on a sunny spring day at 2:00 p.m., could be heard the sound of the simultaneous turning of the pages of the text, Pirates and Pathfinders, in every grade five in the city and province.

Special needs / individual differences

There was little official provision for individual differences in pupils. Teachers, however,

were skilled in meeting the individual needs of each. Discipline was fairly strict. Corporal punishment was part of the school life. Pupils who did not meet the standard were "failed". It was only much later that we began to question whether the child "failed", or we "failed" the child.

"We simply taught those who showed up."

In my first five years of teaching, with one dramatic exception, I taught no pupils with very special needs. The exception was the influx into the city of Toronto of a large number of immigrants, mostly from Italy. This happened in my third year of teaching and increased my class of thirty-four to fifty-two. Most pupils spoke no English, no special programmes or materials were available to help us meet the needs of these young people. We were totally unprepared for their arrival.

What did we do? We simply accepted each of them and did our best to help them learn and grow. We did not attempt to remove them to a "special place". We did not attempt to exclude them from our classes and schools. In the best tradition of public education, "we simply taught those who showed up". We did our best; they learned. They did well; they enriched this country. To this day, I remember many of these children by name. Although at that time I was totally oblivious of the concept, this was my first experience of "Each Belongs".

Appointed Principal: an interesting school

St. Paul's Boys' School was situated in the inner city of Toronto. I was appointed principal in 1956. Poverty was the norm, abuse and neglect in the community was not unknown. The population was transient. The school was administered by the Brothers of the Christian Schools. Their vocation was to teach poor boys. They made no undue allowance for the social difficulties faced by their pupils. They expected their pupils to learn, and they did. They wished their pupils to continue their academic learning in high school, and they did, even at a time when schooling beyond elementary school was not guaranteed, or even seen as necessary for all children.

When we started, none of us knew what the end would be. If we had to set down our outcomes before we started, we never would have predicted what did happen, or worse still, we may have limited the possibilities.,

Betty Browne
Superintendent of Student Services

What emerged was a simple yet profound idea, that all children had equal rights to participate in a daily round of school life as fully as possible; they all belong, each belonged.

Peter Burns
Superintendent

At recess time, the junior opportunity class played among themselves, and so did the senior opportunity kids. There was no interaction between the "opportunity children" and the rest of the school population.

Joyce D. Puckerin
Teacher

Although the official policy of the time was to make "special arrangements" for inner city public school pupils, fewer than forty percent of the graduates of Duke of York School, a neighbour to St. Paul's and the showcase of inner city programmes, chose further academic learning. At the same time eighty-five percent of the Brothers' boys from St. Paul's, without special programmes, attended high school and many completed university.

My first experience of "integration" was at St. Paul's in 1956. The pupils in the Academic Vocational Class (Senior Opportunity) were included for various reasons in the intermediate division classes.

Catholic High Schools

It is hard to believe that, in 1956, no free Catholic Secondary Education was available in Toronto. Two Brothers, against all odds, opened the only free Catholic High School in Toronto, across the street from St. Paul's. The school grew initially from grades 9 and 10 to encompass each level. The expectation that the students would be diligent and successful was fulfilled. De La Salle Intermediate, as it was called, included the "poor" in Catholic Education. One of the two founders of this school, Jack McAleese, was later a valued principal in the Hamilton Wentworth Catholic School system.

These examples unconsciously developed in me a mind set of inclusion, a suspicion of specialists and experts, and a belief that we were each more alike than different. These experiences also shaped my belief and determined my actions as a teacher and my influence as principal and superintendent. Inevitably, they led me towards "Each Belongs".

Educational reform and social policy change

However, let it be clear, no one person can bring about profound change in education or social policy. If given the opportunity, one person can bring together others of similar hopes and aspirations. It is helpful if that person is in a position of influence and authority.

While it is true that some profound changes came about by happenstance, as we shall see,

This was the beginning of the era to promote students along with their peers and individualize their learning to meet their needs. Our Board embraced this philosophy, not just for the mainstream, but for all students.

Trish Bonney
Resource Teacher
Students who are Deaf/Blind

You have set about a very big task.

Peter Burns
Superintendent

the 1969 Special Service Committee Report provided a more direct, planned and rational opportunity for change.

The context for change

How, in 1969, did the Hamilton Separate School Board its principals, teachers, parents and children, transform a system of separate special programmes and sporadic provision into a fully inclusive education system, where each child truly belonged?

In order to understand the answer to this question, we need to know something of the educational and social background of the times. The story of this achievement was not written, it was lived. Its telling shows us the purposes, challenges, values, excitement and joy of learning, whoever we are and wherever we live.

For most of their early history, schools in Ontario and, indeed, in most of the world, were intended for those decreed capable of "profiting from education." Both in policy and function schools welcomed some children and excluded others. In Ontario, school boards, with the advice of the Ministry of Education inspectors, ruled on the admission or the exclusion of children with disabilities. There did not appear to be any right of appeal against their rulings.

Even in the context of the times many of the reasons for exclusion did not make much sense. Physical disabilities, which had no effect on intellectual learning, accounted for many exclusions. For example a lack of toilet training was considered a legitimate reason for exclusion from school. It is possible, if not probable, that at some time in the past a potential doctoral scholar with a physical disability or a lack of bladder control was excluded from school and thus, his/her potential classmates were deprived of rich shared learning experiences.

These decisions were not made by unfeeling or cruel people. They were, however, made by individuals whose vision of education was narrow and did not allow for much beyond the three

In 1966, when I came to Canada, for such children to be in the regular school would have been unthinkable. The attitude has changed dramatically.

G. Ferguson
Principal

How could a behaviourally challenged person experience "normality" in a setting where all children have the same challenges and difficulties?

Eugene Mazur
Principal

We remembered how it felt at the Christmas School Concert when the special children were paraded out like a pitiful clutch of castaways at the end of the concert.

Jan Burke-Gaffney
Parent

"Rs": reading, writing and arithmetic. Those teaching in Catholic schools included the fourth "R": religion.

Some of the larger school boards did offer specialized programmes for slow learners, but they were not designed to prepare them for further education. They provided "Life Skills" and, frequently, custodial programmes. Others offered programmes for slow learners within their schools. Provincial residential schools provided programmes for the blind and the deaf. Seemingly greater significance was attached to the special "need" of the child than to the contribution of the young person's family and community life to his/her growth and development.

Labels were at best pejorative but more frequently brutal, with persons being labelled morons, idiots, or imbeciles. Similar labels were commonplace in the UK, often based on IQ tests and quotients. Special schools were labelled "Schools for the Trainable Retarded". The first of these schools was parent founded, funded and run. In England similar schools were called "junior training centres" for the "subnormal". Pupils attending them were labelled "ineducable", and came under the jurisdiction of Health, and not the Educational authorities. The thinking being that as the children were "ineducable" they did not require schooling.

For the most part, education in Ontario before the 1950's was for the able student. Few were expected to go to university and few did. Jobs were abundant, higher education less compelling. Persons with disabilities were looked after within the family, or large, very segregated, and mostly isolated institutions.

Paradoxically, persons with disabilities who lived in rural or isolated areas were more likely to be included in the community than those who lived in larger, urban areas, with the presumed benefits of access to experts and special facilities.

In the late 1950's and the early 1960's programmes for children with disabilities began to emerge in Ontario schools. Always segregated, these programmes took the form of special classes or schools.

To be honest, I didn't know what to make of this movement to integrate students with special needs into their home schools. On the surface, it appeared to be a terrible idea. However, it soon became clear to all of us that this was indeed the way to go.

Dr. Clinton Davis
Head of Psychological Services

Our area was the basement of the school and that in itself probably says something about the times.

Mary Galarneau
Principal of Programmes
Special Education

We lobbied the government for equal consideration for Catholic children, but we were ignored.

P.J. Brennan
Emeritus Director of Education

Catholic schools offered little for children with special educational needs and nothing for those with more severe disabilities. It is sad that the very children who ensured the Catholicity of schools – the Poor of the Gospel - were excluded.

Those children and young people who could not see or could not hear, or who were physically disabled, were not present in the schools. Their absence was blamed on lack of money, an invalid excuse that continues to be cited even today.

Prior to 1969 Hamilton had developed some services which could be considered as special education. For instance, the Ontario Ministry of Education required each school board to recruit one or more "truant officers." Hamilton also appointed two Special Education consultants - one to assist with English as a Second Language (ESL), the other to assess children for placement in "opportunity classes" and provide advice for their teachers. There were also part-time classes for immigrant children who did not speak English.

This phase also witnessed the emergence of a programme of segregated "opportunity classes" in Hamilton. Opportunity, or special classes were created for children with significant learning difficulties who were educated apart from their peers in isolated classroom settings. Here they followed a programme of care or "Life Skills". In 1962 four such classes were started, with further classes being introduced in 1964 and 1966, making a total of ten

Significantly, since all agreed that many of the children should not have been in those classes, the idea of integration began to take root.

The school population grew, fuelled by immigration, predominantly from Italy. The educational services provided for the newly arrived children were sparse at best and non-existent at worst. Older children who did not speak English were frequently placed two or three grade levels below their age group, almost inevitably leading to negative socialization and a loss of feelings of self worth. Many immigrant children left school long before secondary school graduation, and those who went to secondary school were frequently screened to segregated

The failure to pass at the end of the year was a marker for the potential destiny of an opportunity class.

Carol Roth
Teacher

The school board at that time was still buying services from the public board for students they felt they were not equipped to handle in their regular school system.

Barbara Italiano
Parent

Jim Hansen is an angry young man with a vision.

told to Eugene Perabo
Coordinator of Special Education

Vocational schools or the two year programmes, aptly named "Terminal Courses".

Paradoxically, and frequently prophetically, those who tended to do well were children who were simply allowed to attend school, received little extra help, and were never placed in special programmes. Less intrusive interventions were developed over the years and children ceased to be in need of special education services simply on the grounds that their first language was not English.

Fortunately in education, as in life, nothing is ever static. The 1950's brought new citizens to the country and to schools. These new citizens and students brought their own special gifts, and in turn, blessed the Hamilton schools and community by introducing their own values, skills, and expectations, to the existing culture. The baby boom had arrived and schooling became more complex and demanding. The educational literature of the late 1950's and early 1960's addressed such developments as un-graded schools, "schools without failure", and child centred education.

A further significant step forward was the publication, in 1968, of the Hall-Dennis Commission Report "For the Love of Learning". Education was beginning to be seen as more than schooling, while the burgeoning integration movement for racial equality also did much for the needs of minority groups and, in particular, for those with disabilities.

On June 10th, 1965 the Government of Ontario established a Provincial Committee on Aims and Objectives of Education in the Schools of Ontario. "Living and Learning", the report of the Provincial Committee, was published in June of 1968. The 258 recommendations of "Living and Learning" impacted education in Ontario as had no previous report.

This impact was due to the overriding concern of members of the Provincial Committee with the need for Ontario to turn from its existing educational approach focused on teachers, testing, and tradition to a future focus on the child, learning, and individualization.

Jim Hansen made it his mission to teach all of us that every child should have the opportunity to be in our schools with their brothers and sisters.

Rita Ricottone
Special Education Resource Teacher

Though 258 separate recommendations were made, the Committee considered that there was one underlying key recommendation that the Government must:

Establish, as fundamental principles governing school education in Ontario,

a) the right of every individual to have equal access to the learning experience best suited to his needs, and

b) the responsibility of every school authority to provide a child-centred curriculum that invites learning by individual discovery and inquiry.

"Living and Learning" created a wind of change felt in every school system in Ontario. Nowhere was the wind of change felt more keenly and with more meaning than in the Hamilton-Wentworth Catholic District School Board. Only in HWCDSB were the terms "equal access, child-centred" extended to all learners, abled and disabled alike.

Chapter 3

Blocks to Growth and Inclusion

There are blocks to the growth of our children, able and disabled. Some are to be found within our schools, our educational policies and practice. Others have their origins within the wider community. Yet all are within our power to control or change.

If the image that we have of ourselves is a reflection of what others think of us, whose negative image is being reflected to those who have come to doubt their ability? What are we doing in our multi-million dollar institutions that cause little children, who begin certain of their ability and worth, to become doubters?

If the school is to foster growth in all children, able and disabled, we must be aware of our awesome power to help shape a positive self-image in each child.

Testing

Testing has become a pervasive factor in the lives of teachers and pupils alike. In my experience, there are essentially two types of tests used in schools and school boards; tests that evaluate and tests that measure.

Teacher tests

Teacher-made tests, or quizzes as they are sometimes called, measure the content of what a child has learned from a lesson or a series of lessons. They have always been with us and are useful to both teacher and pupil. The results of the quiz help the teacher identify which of the material needs re-teaching, and which needs re-inforcement. For the pupil, he/she becomes aware of those areas that need further study. These tests support good teaching.

We met and he proceeded to instruct me on the basics of C. P. and the ramifications of the disorder to the education process. I left the meeting with meaningless information which had little reference to my teaching.
Tony DeMarco
Special Education Resource Teacher

I also remember my younger brother having a lot of difficulty in Grade 1. Every paper he brought home had a great big X across it.
Karen Moyer
Special Education Resource Teacher

The school psychology model that was in vogue at the time emphasized psycho-educational assessments of students as a vehicle for placement in special education classes.
Dr. Clinton Davis
Head of Psychological Services

I.Q. tests

Tests that attempt to measure innate qualities of a person have also been with us a very long time. Intelligence tests, for example, claim to be able to assign an I.Q. (Intelligence Quotient) to persons taking the test. Some I.Q. tests attempt to sample verbal ability, others are mainly non-verbal. Tests may be administered individually, to groups, or to the whole class. The scores are often arbitrarily labelled or categorized. Children scoring between 85 to 115 are generally assigned to the 'average' group and regarded as 'normal'. If a society equates 'normal' with 'average', who would want to be 'normal'? Children may also be labelled 'gifted', 'dull normal', or 'retarded' on the basis of their test scores.

These tests and categories continue to this day to be applied to children in many school boards and education authorities. The negative affects of the tests on so many borders on the criminal.

An introductory psychology course tells us that a test must have validity and reliability. Test validity describes the extent to which a test genuinely measures what it claims to measure, e.g. intelligence.

Test reliability describes its consistency. If the test is taken on several occasions by the same population you should get consistently similar results. Of course, this may not necessarily be 'valid', and your 'I.Q.' test may in fact be measuring other characteristics of the child, such as short-term memory, culture, or enthusiasm for that type of educational experience.

However, since there is no consensus among psychologists about the definition of intelligence, how can we possibly measure it and why would we bother to try?

Some children, over the years, have been refused admittance to school on the grounds of their I.Q. test score. Even today, in some administrations, children are refused admission to the neighbourhood school on these grounds. Grade 8 graduates were frequently assigned to their

No I.Q. measure can really tell us the full potential of a child - not really.
Ella Lorincz
Resource Teacher, Developmental Disabilities

Today, children with special needs are not just accepted into their neighbourhood schools, they are active, involved, and most of all, productive members of their school communities. They continue to have their own unique strengths and weaknesses and work hard every day to attain their goals.
Karen Moyer
Special Education Resource Teacher

High School streams, Advanced, Basic and General, on the result of group I.Q. test scores.

Abolition of I.Q. testing in Hamilton

In the early nineteen-seventies, we forbade the use of group I.Q. tests in the schools of the Hamilton Wentworth Separate School Board. Components of individual I.Q. tests are used rarely, and only with the expressed permission of the Chairman of Psychological Services. Numerical scores are never used. Why, despite the knowledge that these tests are invalid and biased, are they still used? Perhaps the parents of children mislabelled by these tests should seek redress.

Standard Tests

Other standardized tests in common use in schools across the world are not as repugnant as I.Q. tests. They do not categorize children. They claim to measure a pupil's knowledge of certain subject matter, and assign a rank order of achievement to those who complete the test. These tests seem innocent enough, they pass the test of validity and reliability, and they are not used directly to 'justify' exclusion of pupils, as are I.Q. tests. They share with all standardized tests an acceptable margin of error. For 'good' tests, the margin of error is between 6% and 12%. Would you have confidence in a Doctor whose diagnosis record showed a similar margin of error? When given as a diagnostic tool and not scored for grade or percentile level, tests can be helpful.

Misuse of standardized tests

Unfortunately standardized tests have become the vehicle for accountability and the main plank in the education platform of political parties in North America and Europe. The government of Ontario is part of this group. This simple, seemingly effective and non-threatening practice has had, and continues to have, a profoundly negative effect on the growth and development of the children in schools where these tests are used.

Take chances.

Tony DeMarco
Special Education Resource Teacher

We believed then and still do that "every child can learn", so let us give them that opportunity, let us treat them with respect, letting them know we truly believe that they can learn.

Joyce D. Puckerin
Teacher

I believe that Brebeuf did become the first high school to integrate special needs students.

Len Varrasso
Principal

State and Province wide testing programmes

External tests are mandatory in Grades 3 and Grade 6 in Ontario junior schools, and are being extended to secondary schools. Initially, external testing was to be used to get a "big picture" view of competence in certain subject areas across the province. Promises were made that the scores of individual pupils and schools would remain confidential. There would be no comparisons between schools and boards. We have seen all these promises broken. Newspapers in every city publish school-by-school results, supplied to them by the Ministry of Education. Comparisons are made; judgments are passed on the ability of the pupils and by extension, the competence of the principals and teachers.

Most of us in our high school and university life experienced the stress of a formal examination. The examinations were generally two or three hours in length and never given five days in succession. Imagine the pressure placed on our eight year old pupils who sit exams for two and half hours a day, each day for a week. On their shoulders rest the reputation of the teacher, the school and the board. It is truly abusive to require this of these pupils. The abuse is compounded by the requirement that the teacher not answer questions posed by the children during the examination time. What sense do children make of this? What impact does it have on their trust of the teacher? Why do parents allow this abuse?

School funding and the misuse of tests

In some USA states, federal funding is increased or reduced on the basis of school test results. Against all logic, schools that score poorly have their funds reduced. All of this because of flawed tests of reading, maths or sciences. All of this in order to get information that any competent teacher could have supplied, more accurately, without the tests.

Effects of testing on the balanced curriculum

The school curriculum at any grade level must reflect more than reading, writing and math. Most of us would expect our schools to provide courses in music, art, physical education, reli-

I have read that we cannot make assumptions about students; we learn that whatever preconceived notions we have about their capabilities can be broken in a matter of moments.
John Miller
Teacher

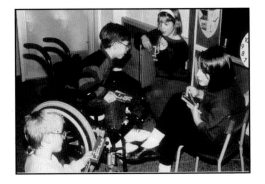

I couldn't understand how a child could fail and be retained in kindergarten already labelled as a failure at the tender age of 5.
Angela Federico
Teacher

gious knowledge, science and social studies. The school's role is also to foster relationships and independent thinking. There is a clear risk under the present system that what is not tested will not be valued. Music, art, drama, school plays, physical education, the arts, extra curricular activities and clubs: none of these is subject to outside accountability. Are they, therefore, to be less valued? Any school that values only the '3Rs' is not a good school.

Tests as a threat to trust in education

Teachers, if they are permitted and trusted to teach, will ensure that each child grows. Teachers have no difficulty in being held accountable for the growth of each pupil. They would, however, prefer not be part of the big lie of that accountability being defined through tests. As educators we know that standardized tests are faulty and that their focus is narrow. We also know that these tests cannot measure excellence, and that they are abusive to children. Why the silence? We will only have true accountability in education when we respect and trust teachers.

Labels as a block to growth

When we label children we impose a block on their growth. Yet we live in a world surrounded by labels. Some labels are so well known that they increase the worth of some lines of clothing. Others keep us safe by warning of dangerous substances or situations. Labels let us know the best and safest times to use the contents of a can or box. For the most part, for example when they deal with goods, services and products, labels may be both positive and helpful. They become less useful and potentially harmful when they are attached to people.

Use and abuse of labels in education

In education, for the most part, we use labels to describe a deviation from what is perceived as a 'normal' performance, achievement, attitude or behaviour. Unfortunately the label soon becomes attached to the child and not to the deficit. For instance, in secondary schools, where students are commonly divided into the streams, Advance, General and Basic,

Teachers learned that reading and arithmetic were not quite as important as the life long values their children were learning by not only accepting but helping and developing friendships with a "special needs child".

Rita Ricottone
Special Education Resource Teacher

The fact that teachers were trusted, and thus shared in the development and implementation stages of curriculum contributed to good teacher morale.

Sister Claudia
Principal

These kids had several strikes against them; emotional, sexual or physical abuse, developmental delay, disadvantaged home, etc., but while they were at St. Theresa's, they were all integrated into regular classes and were , for the most part, very successful.

Tina Travale
Department Head, Special Education

I have been privileged to integrate several special needs students who have been visually challenged or hearing impaired, autistic, Down Syndrome, and physically challenged.

Fred Susi
Teacher

a student is often referred to as a 'basic', rather than as 'a student who is following a 'basic' programme'. It is hard to imagine a teenage student welcoming being labelled 'General' or 'Basic', anymore than we would ourselves.

Effects of labelling on individuality

When we attach the label to the child and not the deficit it is easy for us to forget or deny the individuality of the child. If we talk about 'Downs' children or 'behaviour' children or blind children, or gifted children, we deny their individuality. To recognize and preserve that individuality we might say: 'Mary is a child who has Down Syndrome and she is different from Patrick who also has Down Syndrome. Steve, who is blind, is very different from John who is also blind.' Children with disabilities share with us pride in our own uniqueness. The use of deficit labels in education describes no individual child that lives or has ever lived.

Labels and social attitudes

In Canada and USA, the label 'mentally retarded', still frequently based on I.Q., scores, is further subdivided into 'trainable' and 'educable retarded'. Presumably, children labelled 'trainable retarded' are not seen as likely to benefit from academic learning and are therefore denied the opportunity. Not surprisingly, their educational and social development is severely restricted. In days gone by, children with Down Syndrome were automatically labelled 'mentally retarded'. However, when included in the daily routine of their homeroom in the neighbourhood school, they learned to speak, write and develop skills that had been considered unattainable for them. Today, many young people with Downs syndrome work in our schools. We see them appearing as actors on our television screens. They hold down regular jobs. Their genetic makeup has not changed. What has altered, significantly, is the attitude towards them within our society. We thank the efforts of the young people themselves, their parents, teachers, friends and others for helping to bring this about.

Jim, I really can't think of many obstacles that should block or impede students with special needs in schools other than ATTITUDE.

Carol Cooper
Teacher

Many came to hear and see the "Hamilton Catholic's Board integration" in action. Foremost, the skeptics came to get the recipe and/or find the flaws. The answer remained consistent. It was all a matter of spirit, commitment, vision, creative problem-solving, planning, organization, and energy.

Jackie Bajus
Superintendent of Student Services

Advocacy for segregated settings

The most common deficit label in education is that of 'Learning Disabilities'. 'The Association of Children with Learning Disabilities' is an advocacy group that lobbies vigorously for segregated settings for those of our children who have Learning Disabilities. It is true that many children and adults have difficulty in spelling and penmanship which appear to be innate. These difficulties may be linked to Learning Disabilities. There are also other characteristics attributed to Learning Disabilities that make life difficult for some. The label itself, however, does nothing to alleviate these difficulties. Nor does the literature contain any definition of a 'Learning Disability' with which we can all agree. Wouldn't it be easier for us to recognize the person's difficulties and offer the appropriate support without the negative connotation of the label?

The dangers of attaching funding to pupil labels

Labels sometime exist and persist because they attract special funding. For instance, a major change in the funding formula in the United States of America provided more money for children identified as Learning Disabled than for those labelled as Trainable Retarded. It was no great surprise when we witnessed a rapid decline in the number of children labelled as Retarded! This decline was a direct result of the change in the formula which rewarded the labelling of children as 'Learning Disabled.'

I remember saying, at a Ministry meeting with other school board supervisors, "We have this young lady who has Down Syndrome. Therefore she's retarded. And she reads and writes, does gymnastics and French. Now my problem is, what do we call her? Do we call her trainable retarded or educable retarded?" I paused, chuckled, then added, "Actually, we call her Denise."

Our social butterfly was a young girl with Spina Bifida who just loved being around other kids and exuded such a positive, sunny attitude that her disability and wheelchair were seldom seen as impediments for taking an active part in the group.

Ella Lorincz
Resource Teacher, Developmental Disabilities

I remember thinking how "impossible" the job would be and yet how stimulating and inspiring it would be to challenge myself to do it.

Ann Stevenson
Speech Pathologist

Labels provide no guidance for teaching children

There are many common labels we use to describe children whose behaviour presents challenges. Autism, a poorly understood condition and label, is employed to describe a syndrome of unusual behaviours and communication patterns. It is sometimes subsumed under the heading of P.D.D. (Pervasive Development Disorder) or, A.D.S (Attention Deficit Syndrome).

Labels do not give guidelines for action. Nor are they educationally based. Sometimes they are used, mistakenly, to justify and excuse inappropriate behaviours. My view is that children who consistently exhibit them, at home, school or in the larger community, must learn to modify or eliminate them. If they do not their lives will be unhappy and unproductive. Helping children to learn how to behave more appropriately is difficult but not impossible. It is one of our tasks, as educators, to accomplish this without threat to their feelings of self-worth. It is self-defeating and ineffective for a government to allocate funding for labels. Money should be provided for individual planning and support needs. Teachers don't need the label to help the child.

Early failure as a block to growth

Early failure is a block to growth. There is no escaping failure – for any of us - in our daily activities. The bread does not always rise, the putt doesn't always drop and stock markets decline. These often add spice to our lives.

We also recognize the presence of failures or harmful experiences that impair a child's growth and development. Many of these, for example school failure or grade retention, are within our hands to avoid. In the not so distant past, grade retention was quite common. Boys were failed more frequently than girls, the children of the poor more often than those of the rich, 'immigrant' children almost automatically. The reasons for 'failure' were arbitrary, sometimes punitive and invariably illogical.

Harmful effects of 'retention' on a pupil's growth

In the 1950's, elementary pupils who achieved less than 50% average on all subjects were retained. Pupils who achieved more than 50% on average but less than 50% in either mathematics or reading were retained. Presumably a pupil with an 85% average overall could have

For me, the most notable accomplishment for our system was the integration of the children from the Developmental Centre into our system at Our Lady of Lourdes School in 1983.

Pat Zettel
Coordinator of Programs, Special Education

Through the acceptance of this basic right, children who had not been considered as members of the school community were now being welcomed at the doors.

Carol Roth
Teacher

Little Jason came to Vera Kerry's classroom, having sat in his playpen; he did not communicate or walk. By the end of the year, she had him walking, running, laughing-grunting, and toilet trained.

Sister Martina
Teacher

been retained because of a 49% in Math. Secondary school students who achieved less than 50% in two subjects were retained. Students required to repeat a year, at elementary or secondary level, started over in all subject areas, including those they had already successfully completed. Does this seem logical to you?

Only after a considerable passage of time was the damage caused by retention recognized. Study after study indicated that 'failing' a student did not improve his or her academic achievement. In fact it did the opposite. Any benefits of grade repetition were far outweighed by the negative or harmful effects. While the burden of proof was on the advocates to justify retention, its practice continued in many school boards.

There are so many effective teaching techniques we can use to help students achieve that it becomes almost unprofessional to counsel or allow retention. Children, able and disabled alike, of four or five years of age in Early Childhood Education or Kindergarten should never be retained. Had they stayed at home until they were five they would have entered directly into grade one. Early Childhood Education and Kindergarten students with a disability are sometimes retained because they "are not mature enough". We should remind ourselves before making such life decisions that it is the function of four or five year olds to be immature! One does not learn to be a six year old by being with five year olds.

Segregation and pupil development

Segregation is a block to growth. We have discontinued segregating our children on the grounds of colour or ethnicity. This practice, more prevalent in the United States than in Canada, led to a devaluing of those persons who were segregated. The segregation of children in our schools on the basis of race or colour is against the law. Segregating school children on the grounds of disability, real or perceived, is still permitted and in many boards and education authorities is the norm rather than the exception.

If you live in the area,
you can come to your school.

John Miller
Teacher

Forget the handicap, disregard the label, look beyond the chair, see through the slurred words, go beyond the silence, and discover the real person.

Tony DeMarco
Special Education Resource Teacher

When Pietro was going into his last three years of elementary school, he moved from St. Michael's, to Blessed Kateri, along with his principal, Toni Tigani, and was enrolled in a regular grade 6 class. This was the end of the General Learning Disability classes in the elementary schools.

Barbara Italiano
Parent

A segregated school placement is seldom freely chosen: it is generally imposed and is always harmful. At present, in many boards, if you can read, write and calculate, or it is believed you can read, write and calculate, you will be placed in your neighbourhood school where you will learn to read, write and calculate and will be properly socialized. If you cannot read, write and calculate, or if it is believed you cannot read, write and calculate, you will be placed in a special school or class where you will not learn to read, write and calculate and will not have an opportunity for proper socialization. Where is the socialization? What can compensate for example of "regular" or "able" children?

The segregation of children with disabilities is unjust because it reduces their opportunities for learning. Segregation of children with disabilities is based on a promise of greater care, safety and opportunity for learning. It is a false promise. The reality of segregation is lower standards, fewer expectations, and a 'once and for all placement'.

Acquiring Language

How long will it take us to realize that you can't put together all the children who can't speak in a segregated classroom in order that they learn to speak? It is called a language class and only the teacher speaks. Just beyond the closed door of the "language class" are hundreds of teachers of language: the *other children*.

A child's entitlement to be educated alongside peers

Each child is entitled to the full range of experiences offered through public education, including the opportunity of interaction with others able and disabled alike. Children learn from their teachers and each other. Children at school bring their own unique experiences, strengths, weaknesses and values to the groups. Each has something to give and something to gain. We rise to the level of our group.

Could they not start in a typical class and work their way out?

Phil DiFrancesco
Superintendent of Student Services
quoting Marsha Forest

It is full inclusion that makes available many possibilities for each exceptional student with special needs to be fully alive.

Aldona Hubbard
Teacher

Neighbourhood schools – the rightful place for meeting pupil needs

Some children need special equipment and help from people with special skills. However, we have found that whatever can, or needs to be done in a segregated setting, can be replicated in the neighbourhood school. The presence of the specialized equipment, skilled professionals, and teaching assistants that may be necessary for the child with a disability, also enhance the learning experience for able pupils. Neighbourhood schools where pupils with disabilities are accepted and included are safer and more peaceful.

Those who support the provision of small, segregated groups of similarly labelled people as a viable learning environment, need to provide the evidence to justify that viewpoint.

The rights of all children, able and disabled

From the very beginning of our journey, we have equally championed the rights of able children to a good and complete education. They have the right to interact with those who are different from themselves. A right to the joy that comes from witnessing or even helping a person with a disability, against great odds, succeed.

The witness of those with disabilities tells the able that they need not be perfect to be loved, honoured and respected. The 'able' students should not be segregated from those with disabilities; they have as much right to a complete education as their disabled classmates.

Principals, if you wish a happy, peaceful, caring environment where learning thrives, my message to you is to seek out and welcome into your school, the children in your neighbourhood who are in some way disabled. You, your staff and your community will be forever changed.

Blocks to inclusion are the most damaging because they are placed in the path of learning by other persons. However, they can just as easily be removed. Just do it! Just let the children in! Just change attitudes! Growth is blocked when inclusion is blocked.

That a school principal would listen to and talk with all the students and their parents with kindness, understanding and genuine empathy instead of coming with the proverbial big stick struck me as amazing. This is when I started to realize that "Each Belongs".

Les Galambos
Principal of Special Education

I remember the smile on Stacey's face when she heard my voice. Or the waving arms of excitement of other non-verbal students when I spoke to them and joked with them .

Frank Goodman
Principal

It was your vision and mission on behalf of the special needs children of Hamilton-Wentworth that led to the creation of inclusive policies and the philosophy "Each Belongs".

Jerry Ponikbar
Emeritus Director of Education

Blocks to Inclusion

Justice, not charity

Just as there are threats and blocks to growth, there are also "Blocks to Inclusion". While blocks to growth arise for the most part from practices and procedures, the blocks to inclusion are more a function of attitude. Practices and procedures are easier to change than attitudes. However, we must not allow the problems of bringing about attitude change to determine whether or not a child attends, and is a full member of, his or her local school.

As I have pointed out in earlier chapters, inclusion is not about charity. It is a matter of justice, of human rights. Justice is not, in our society, a commodity we need to 'shop around' to find. Justice is ours by right. Justice demands that each child be included in the neighbourhood school. Justice does not guarantee that perfection or even excellence will be found there; it does guarantee that each will share equally in the experiences the school provides.

Parents' pioneering role in the development of services for children

Not so long ago there was little or no provision of service for children with disabilities. These children were seldom present in our schools and frequently hidden from society. Parents, without supports, either cared for their son or daughter at home or placed them in large impersonal institutions. That is no longer the case. Thanks to the determined actions of individuals and groups of parents working together, with little external help, we have seen radical change in the years that followed.

Parental fears

These parents are to be honoured as pioneers. When there was no place for a child, they provided one. Understandably, the programs and placements were always segregated and generally unsophisticated. Most parents welcomed the developments which occurred in the placements and programmes over the years for children with disabilities. Some didn't. But the process of

I can recall teachers and principals literally reeling in terror at the thought of adding children, who had a variety of disabilities with which they were totally unfamiliar, and felt unprepared to help the children with their special problems.

John Grosso
Superintendent In-Service Training

I still remember the staff meeting where I presented Bill 82 (Right to Education Bill in Ontario) and tried to alleviate the fears of the classroom teachers. There were so many questions and so few answers at that time.

Frank Goodman
Principal

I remember the initial opposition, in the early 1970's to the inclusion of special needs students; opposition from parents, and principals, and staff.

Frank Goodman
Principal

Father O'Leary made some offhand comment about how the Board has all of us "brainwashed" about inclusion and that it didn't really work in a real classroom.

Steve Travale
Educational Assistant, Teacher

change was not a criticism of the past. We owe thanks to the work of those dedicated 'pioneers' who overcame the blocks – and blocks there were – while pointing the way to the future and the beginnings of inclusion.

Fear as a block to inclusion

The first block to overcome on the journey to inclusion is "Fear". Many of those pioneering parents had found comfort in the programmes and placements of the day. Their sons/daughters were cared for by good people, in a safe place. Talk of de-institutionalizing, de-segregation, individual programming, school attendance, independent living - all created anxiety. Having worked so hard to find a safe place for their son/daughter most feared the changes. It is important that we learn from our history. The greatest honour we pay to the pioneers mentioned above, is to help their programmes change and grow. We must never forget that our determination for children with disabilities to be included grew out of their determination to have a special place for their children.

It is true to say that the beginning of inclusion did not meet with universal parental approval - many feared a loss of the security and safety their child's placement provided. Many feared that their child would not be welcomed into a "normal" setting. Care, security and safety were, and still are, the reasons behind segregated placements. Despite the advent of well-funded and staffed programmes in mainstream schools, parents' anxieties continued. Would their child be accepted? Would the 'other' children make fun of them? Would they present an unmanageable burden for the teacher? Would teachers and pupils be part of the process of accepting children with disabilities into their school? All had to deal with their fears. Could they, as teachers, meet the needs of these children? How would the other children react? How would the parents of the 'other' children react? Would there be sufficient resources?

The philosophy and indeed the spirituality of "Each Belongs" have influenced the wider community and made it more aware of the dignity of every human being.

Anthony Cushieri/Jerry Creedon
Religion Teachers

I am convinced that inclusion is the proper way to proceed. I believe that its success is dependent on the proper resources and supports being available.

Des Brennan
Supervisor, Social Services

"Truly inclusive community" are only words unless they are lived every day.

Barbara Italiano
Parent

True, she was different, but perhaps not as different as some of the other kids in the room were different.

Mr. J. Hogan
Teacher

I had to stop and say "Whoa! Why?" because at that time I believed these children were best served in a specific protected environment where "specialists" could provide the best program in a segregated setting that was not really academic. Boy, was I ever wrong!!

Eugene Mazur
Principal

Growth entails risk

The genuine anxieties and fears of the parents, pupils and teachers were and are real threats to inclusion. And it is important for us, as educators to listen and discuss.

The growth that we seek, that children need and deserve, will not occur without risk. Children must be permitted to risk. Parents and teachers must set aside their unreasonable fears and set the terms and conditions of permissible risk. It seems to me that each of us could follow the same advice. Set aside our own unreasonable fears, determine our life goals, evaluate the risks, and set the terms and conditions for dealing with that risk. No risk, no growth.

Lack of knowledge as a threat to inclusion

Many of the blocks to inclusion are based on a lack of knowledge. Inclusion in schools does not mean everybody doing the same things at the same time and in the same way. Inclusion does not mean ten year olds with six year olds. Inclusion cannot take away disabilities nor does it promise or require 'curing' anyone. Inclusion is not a programme or a placement.

How do I define what inclusion is? Inclusion is a state of being. We cannot have partial inclusion. That is a contradiction. Inclusion of exceptional children is not a burden to the school; it is a joy! Inclusion is a guarantee that each child, able and disabled alike, will share in the best possible education, with its highs and lows, that our skills and resources allow.

I remember what it was like to be a misfit refugee coming to a strange country, not understanding or speaking the language, which became a social barrier. I did not care for the labels that set me apart in the class.

Ella Lorincz
Resource Teacher, Developmental Disabilities

Prejudice as a threat to inclusion

Pre-judgment and prejudice are both blocks to inclusion. In fact, they are often the main reason for segregating or excluding children with disabilities. We define pre-judgment as, "to judge without knowing all the facts," while a prejudice is 'an opinion or judgment, generally negative, based on irrelevant consideration or inadequate knowledge.'

We would be wrong to assume that anyone expressing prejudicial views is necessarily acting from malice or ill-will. They may well believe they are acting in the best interests of the young person with disabilities. Or that inclusion is against the best interests of the majority of pupils in a school or class. This 'well intentioned' but prejudicial opinion, often seen as a genuine expression of concern, is more difficult to recognize for what it is. Direct, outspoken prejudice is more easily confronted. It is important that more subtle prejudice, hidden, perhaps even from ourselves, be brought to light, confronted and corrected.

Over a period of twenty-three years as superintendent, I had numerous opportunities to run workshops and make presentations to parents and professionals from many different disciplines. At the start of a session, I would sometimes ask the audience to assist me in a research project. They were each given a list of thirty names identified as children in Grade 4 at St. Lawrence School in Hamilton. The task of the audience was to divide the thirty pupils into three reading groups, A-B-C, or more creatively, bicycles, tricycles and unicycles. When the task was completed the papers were collected without comment.

The class and its pupils did not exist. Angelo Dianni, the principal of St. Lawrence and I made up the names. The list contained Anglo-Saxon names, foreign names, unusual names and names from the newest immigrant group at the school, Italian.

I was amazed to find on the first occasion I presented the task that over 75% of those present completed it. This high percentage of response was repeated presentation after presentation. And the results? We generally found that children with Italian names were often represented in the lowest level of reading. Children with Anglo-Saxon names usually predominated in the top group.

Why had so many mature, learned and often professional people completed a complex test in the absence of any significant information? Why did so few refuse? How, out of the heads and hearts of these good people, did the stereotypes emerge?

I remember seeing representatives from Boards across Canada trying to grasp the magic that made our Board so successful.
Irene Repsys
Special Education Resource Teacher

She was able to participate in the Christmas pageant by being one of the angels. She was wheeled on stage by two other angels.
John Skhopiak
Teacher

Clearly, many of us unconsciously harbour prejudices. Equally clearly, for those of us who are educators, these prejudices will disadvantage some of our pupils. The fact that the task assigned was contrived, that it was assigned without warning or context, may have influenced the outcomes. But the activity provided a sharp insight into our beliefs. The evidence of daily experiences confirms that the prejudging of children with disabilities is a frequent occurrence. The fact that it is expressed in some school board and education authority documents and is reflected in the words of some principals and teachers, is unacceptable. We can make amends by being more welcoming.

Exceptional students are not served by sympathy or sentimentality. Rather they need a sense of belonging, reasonable success, and concern for their dignity as persons.
R. Thompson
Teacher, General Learning Disability

Prejudiced thinking about children with disabilities

A label, 'judging without knowledge of all the facts', fits the definition of prejudice. The school placement of a child based on a label is unprofessional.

Over the years, I have been exposed to statements about children with disabilities that I believe reflected prejudgment and prejudice. These statements were frequently used to justify segregated placements. If we want to check whether or not a statement about a child reflects prejudice, apply this simple test; repeat the following statements using different descriptors for the child:

1 (a) Children with disabilities "cause disruptions by their behaviour".
1. (b) Gifted children "cause disruptions by their behaviour".

2.(a) Teachers should have the right to refuse to teach "children with disabilities".
2. (b) Teachers should have the right to refuse to teach "children of colour".

3. (a) Children with disabilities should be "educated with their own kind".
3. (b) Immigrant children, children of colour, aboriginal children should be "educated with their own kind".

Can there be any doubt that each of these statements is offensive and insensitive and limiting to the persons named?

Each of the children in the above list, able and disabled, of colour, of aboriginal descent, gifted, of immigrant parents, are more alike than different. Each is unique and irrepeatable. Decisions about their school programmes and placements must recognize this uniqueness.

Educational thinking reflects individual needs, not personal prejudice. Statements that reflect prejudices towards, race, colour and ethnicity are offensive and unacceptable not only by the law, but also by the standards of decency that we impose on ourselves. Those who are disabled deserve the same respect.

Sentimentality

Nothing that we do for persons with disabilities will be effective if based on sentimentality or pity. Sentimentality is in fact a block to true inclusion in society. Sentimentality is reflected in both words and deeds. "He's not heavy, he's my brother" is a well-known saying. It is a good example of sentiment overcoming reality. If he weighs three hundred pounds he is heavy, whether or not he is your brother.

On the surface there appears to be no malice intended by slogans or sentimental comments about persons with disabilities. Sentimentality, however, allows us to deny or minimize the reality of a disability and its consequences. If a disability is a 'blessing', if parents of a child with a disability are 'blessed by God', if those who work with disability are 'nice', if persons who are blind, deaf, and physically disabled are all friendly and kind and honourable, then there is no real consequence to the disability. We are insulating ourselves from the pain and its restricting effects. Nor are we compelled to recognize the real person and offer meaningful help. The reality is not idyllic; 'just because you are disabled doesn't mean you are nice'. Parents of children with disabilities are not always patient or feeling blessed by God. People who work with and for the disabled are paid for what they do. Whether or not they happen to be 'nice' does not depend on the nature of their work.

Telethons: an example of sentimental thinking

Special Olympics and the Jerry Lewis Telethon are examples of sentimentality on a grand scale. Special Olympics involve mostly persons with developmental delays, formerly known as 'retarded' in Canada and the USA. These persons, adults for the most part, become part of a fantasy. The experience is enjoyable but fleeting. The participants feel good about themselves for the duration of the activities. The sponsors and the volunteers have spent millions of dollars to promote and stage the event; they feel pride in their achievements.

Couldn't we spend that money more productively to provide more lasting benefits and opportunities for the Special Olympians? If the same love, energy and genuine commitment displayed by the volunteers was used to find meaningful employment for these and other persons with disabilities, wouldn't they experience that feeling of worth on a more regular basis? The millions spent on the Special Olympics could provide job coaches and 'job shadow' where needed. The sponsors, the professional athletes, the valued volunteers, would find themselves engaged in a reality many times more satisfying then the fantasy of Special Olympics.

The annual Jerry Lewis Telethon has raised many millions of dollars over the years for "crippled" children. This initiative and its results are unparalleled in the world. However, is it really necessary to use children as objects of pity to enhance giving? The stature and presence of Jerry Lewis should be sufficient. The revenue from telethons should not free governments of their responsibility to care for their citizens. Telethons should provide for the amenities, not the necessities of life.

Though a feeling "from the trenches" was that the Board had perhaps moved too quickly in this direction, its "jumping in feet first" yielded definitely positive results.

Gaiyle Connolly
Art & Religion Teacher

125ᵗʰ Anniversary
Hamilton Diocese   1856-1981

Diocese of Hamilton   Chancery Office, 700 King St. West, Hamilton, ONT L8P 1C7 (416)328-7981

January 11, 1982

Mr. J. A. Hansen
Chairman, Special Education,
Advisory Planning Committee
The Hamilton-Wentworth Roman Catholic
Separate School Board
90 Mulberry St.
P.O. Box 2012
Hamilton, Ont.
L8N 3R9

Dear Mr. Hansen:

I am grateful for the opportunity to address, in the light of the Catholic faith, the implementation of Bill 82 in the ongoing ministry of Catholic education in Hamilton-Wentworth.

This proposal will move from the general to the particular; hopefully it will not prejudice the tasks of those who must oversee the complex details of implementation.

On March 4, 1981, the Holy See issued a document on the "International Year of the Disabled Persons". It is a fine statement of the philosophical principles at stake.

1.)   The church's work with the disabled and handicapped is undertaken in imitation of Jesus Christ. He showed special care for the suffering in His earthly ministry, individuality and totality".

2.)   The exceptional suffering neighbour is to be seen as the "least of Christ's brethren" (cf. Mt. 25:31-46). In these people, "in a mysterious way", is reflected the image and likeness of God.

3.)   Everyone, including the exceptional, has an "unrepeatable value". Each is a fully human subject, with sacred and inviolable rights. This statement is based upon this unique, innate and independent value of the person, a value which man or society does not bestow.

4.)   Societies often place a high value on utility: they are interested in "functional" members. However, "the quality of a society and a civilization are measured by the respect shown to the weakest of its members".

5.)   However many handicapped people there are, they will be a minority group within the community. There is, therefore, the constant danger of exclusion from, the discrimination by, society. Education has an important role to play in countering the "often spontaneous reaction of a community that rejects and psychologically represses that which does not fit into its habits".

THREE GOALS

The Holy See suggests three more practical principles that might usefully guide the Board's efforts:

1.)   The principle of integration opposes the tendency, mentioned above, "to isolate, segregate and neglect" the exceptional.

2.)   The principle of normalization follows from this. It

points to "the achievement of a living and working environment" for the exceptional, "that resembles the normal one as much as possible".

3.) The principle of personalization emphasizes the fact that, in dealing with the exceptional, "it is always the dignity, welfare and total development of the handicapped person, in all his or her dimensions and physical, moral and spiritual faculties, that must be primarily considered, protected and promoted. This principle also signifies and involves the elimination of collectivized and anonymous institutions to which the disabled are sometimes relegated."

PARTICULAR SUGGESTIONS

The statement of the Holy See indicates that
Even the best legislation, however, risks having no effect on the social context and not producing full results if it is not accepted into the personal conscience of the citizens and the collective consciousness of the community.

This would seem to suggest some directions for Board policy:

1.) The formation of personal conscience in this regard will assume priority status. Teachers, it would seem, will have to be trained to see their work with the exceptional as Christian obligation rather than as a "favour" or mere "compliance with Board policy".

Such moral formation must involve all staff, and mot merely those visibly identified as "specialists" in "working with" the exceptional student.

Curricula is religious and family life education must be examined and structured in such a way that they specifically address the poor, suffering and defenseless as those in whom, for the Christian, the face of "God in

Christ is most clearly seen.

2.) The Catholic school has a role to play in forming the "collective consciousness", and conscience, of the community at large. In a way analogous to sacramental preparation programs, this task could involve educational opportunities for parents. It would also seem to imply a highly-visible presence on the part of Catholic educators in community projects directed to the exceptional members of our society.

3.) The formation of conscience in this area demands educational opportunities for staff such that they will have the requisite knowledge for Christian decision-making. Such opportunities will have to include an emphasis on psychology, interaction with the families of exceptional students, availability of community services and their integration with the Catholic school, crisis intervention and, of course, Catholic moral theology.

On January 1, 1981, Pop John Paul II, in his homily for the World Day of Peace, referred to the International Year of the Handicapped. I join my wishes and prayers for the Board's efforts to those which the Holy Father expressed on that occasion:

I hope and trust that under Mary's motherly gaze, experiences of human and Christian solidarity will be multiplied, in a renewed brotherhood that will unite the weak and strong in the common path of the divine vocation of the human person.

Sincerely yours in Christ,

Bishop of Hamilton

Chapter 4

Inclusion:
A *good and complete education for each child*

The purpose of education

There can be no doubt that each child is entitled to a good and complete education; an opportunity, unfortunately, denied to many children with disabilities.

My good fortune to be working in Hamilton provided me with many opportunities to share with parents and others our journey to, and joy in, inclusive education. My message has not been integration, mainstreaming, or even inclusion. It has been, simply, "A Good Education" for each child, able and disabled alike.

My vision of what constitutes a good complete education developed over the years through reflection, varied experiences and the influence of others. After thirty-nine years in education in Ontario, I have come to the conclusion that most of the curriculum learning that we consider important in education is not. Relationships are what really matter. Children learn from their teachers and each other. Each child is different. Each has something to give and something to gain. Relationships are the vehicle for learning and the reason for "Each Belongs".

It follows that my focus is the specific, individual child; not children, not a group or a class. We do not teach children, or a group, or a class. We teach a child. I write about education, not special education. *Special education is a state of mind. It is good teaching. It is not a programme, not a curriculum. It is all programmes and all curricula.*

If we are to talk about education, our starting point should be learning. Some would argue

We made the necessary accommodations but we did not teach to the handicap. We taught to the child and children are the same all over. They want to belong.

Donna Dupuis
Teacher

that a child begins to learn in the womb. Most of us would probably agree that the informal education of the child, able or disabled, begins at birth and is fostered in the family. And there is general agreement that the time between birth and school entry is the period of greatest growth and critical learning in the child's life.

Parents entrust much of the education of their child to society through the schools. They trust that their child will receive a good and complete education. They intend to be more than spectators in the schooling process; to be involved, to be informed, and to give advice. What is this precious gift of education, that we wish for our children?

My experience as a teacher, as a school superintendent and parent, has taught me that education is far more than schooling, academic achievement, or preparation for work. Education has two main components, academic learning and socialization. Each is important, both are valid forms of achievement. While students may not achieve academically at the same level, in the same way, nor at the same time, nevertheless each will achieve.

Education as growth

Let us begin with the basic fact that children must go to school, they have no choice; the government requires it. It follows, therefore, that each child should expect to be welcomed. Too often children with disabilities are excluded from or treated as unwelcome visitors in their own school when they should have a clear hope of a complete education. Children with disabilities are to be no more valued than non-disabled children. They are likewise to be no less valued. Children with disabilities have a prior right to attend the neighbourhood school with their brothers, sisters and friends. A small boy when asked to define "home" answered, "Home is where, when you go there, they have to take you in."

It wasn't until I went to St. Luke's that I had to come to terms with the idea that everybody belongs. It hit me in the face when I arrived there, and learned that three wonderful children had failed kindergarten.

Angelo Frederico
Teacher

Teachers have absolute responsibility to set up, modify, and initiate programs for all students no matter how serious their physical or mental handicaps.

Thomas Stoneburgh
Principal

Schools should be more like home

Since the school exerts such a critical influence on the growth and well-being of the children, it must constantly monitor the effect of its learning, social and pastoral activities on those it cares for. The monitoring we are proposing is more than governmental tests or targets. It has to do with the values, aims and purposes of education. How are teachers to accomplish this? They know that evaluation or accountability in education is subjective and dependent on countless variables. It follows, therefore, that as educators we need a core philosophy. It is on this that we base our actions and accountability.

A personal philosophy

My philosophy of education and learning is growth. To live is to grow. Every child can grow. "Each Belongs". Because he or she is a unique, irrepeatable gift, with something to give, and something to gain, "Each Belongs".

There are many expectations that schools are specifically challenged to meet. Some are very narrow; learning to read, write and calculate, are examples. Others are broader, such as appreciating music and art. Expectations can also reflect practical values, for instance, preparation for employment. Schools are often expected to nurture the spiritual life of the pupils through religious practice and instruction. The range of expectations faced by schools exceeds the number of persons they touch.

Growth as a philosophy of education does not demand that expectations be met in a particular way, at a particular time, or in a particular fashion. However, it does demand growth. The function of the school is to foster personal growth and development. Learning fosters growth. Each of us, including children, able or disabled, learn and grow when we are ready to

Every child was to be included in the scheme of things. Every child was important. Every child could "stand up to be counted".

Sister Francis
Principal

learn. Our readiness comes from having our basic needs met. Learning, in school or at home, is inseparable from our growth and development.

Common needs of pupils and teachers

Teachers and pupils share similar basic needs. The extent to which these needs are met will affect how we learn. What are these basic needs that are so crucial for our growth and well-being? My list is not long. It applies to each person, able or disabled. You may add to or delete from the list if you wish. One cannot, however, either deny or minimize the power of these needs.

The need to belong

The first and most basic need is belonging. When we enter this world, we belong to and are part of the persons who gave us life. We are welcomed into and help form a family. We begin our life journey with others. Throughout our life we guard and expand our "belonging" by forming relationships. We belong to churches, clubs, and schools. We have friends. We have colleagues. The knowledge that we belong is essential to our growth and well-being. In good, successful schools, teachers and pupils share a common experience of belonging. Within the community, those who truly believe that they do not belong often contemplate suicide.

The need to be accepted and valued

The second basic need is to be accepted, to be affirmed. We cannot achieve this alone, and for this we depend on others. To be accepted by another brings comfort and security. To be affirmed goes beyond acceptance, which may be seen as patronizing. Affirmation is life giving. Affirmation is, by dictionary definition, to assert, to confirm, to ratify. The affirmation that we seek comes not from the spoken word, but from the warmth and humanity of our interaction with others.

When those who are significant in our life assert and confirm by their actions that we are

The hostility Sharon exhibited in September and October was almost non-existent. Her sullen countenance changed. She was now one of the group.

Y. Beach
Principal

Through inclusion of exceptional students a bond is established between them and "so-called regular students", so much so that after a period of time, they are no longer viewed as exceptional, but are one of the crowd..

Martin Bates
Teacher

worthy, worthwhile and capable, we blossom. Imagine the effect an affirming teacher has on her pupils, convincing each that they are valued and capable. Imagine the effects pupils have in affirming teachers of their worth. Husbands and wives who affirm each other ensure a lasting, loving relationship. Our shared need, able and disabled alike, to be affirmed and affirming is not simply a pious wish. Our growth and success, our well-being and health flow from it.

The need to succeed

To experience success, on our own terms, is the third basic need. It is not necessary nor even possible to succeed in all that we do. We frequently try activities that challenge us. Some actions may be necessary for our well-being; a job for example. Other activities may be optional and recreational. Whatever the activity, some experience of success is necessary for our well-being. If we continuously fail, we lose heart and give up. Children, in particular, need a healthy measure of success to prepare them for the failures, small and large, that will inevitably occur in their lives. Failure leads to failure. Success leads to success. Children, able and disabled alike, must be helped to build a backlog of success.

The need for challenge vs involuntary competition

The fourth basic need is to be challenged to excellence. The challenge to excel must be related to the age, physical ability, experience and perceived ability of each person. For adults, our challenge to excellence involves doing as well as we can in our daily activities. Teachers and parents must challenge children, particularly children with disabilities, to learn to do things and to do them as well as they are able.

A challenge to excellence has nothing to do with involuntary competition. We are not asking that a child, particularly a child with a disability, 'beat' anyone else at anything. Involuntary

I firmly believe that Debbie benefited from being in her regular school setting. There are, certainly, more positives than negatives to her integration. Most noticeably was her response to her surroundings. When she was in a regular classroom with "regular students" she would behave as she saw them behave.

Cheryl Baldin
Teacher

competition has no place in schools or in society, although those who wish to be part of a competition are perfectly free to do so. Children need to know that excellence comes from effort and that mastery comes from repeated effort. It is particularly important that a child with disabilities experiences the sense of being challenged. Misguided concern or sentimentality should not deflect us from demanding excellence. Not to demand this is to rob a child of a basic need. It is the challenge, not the difficulty of the task, that is needed.

The need to offer service – to contribute

The final need in my short list is the need to offer service to others. Many of us have the good fortune to offer service to others every day through our employment. Opportunities for service are everywhere. Mothers, fathers and children serve each other in the family; priests serve the people in their parishes; police and firemen serve the city; people offer and receive service. We are very good at serving others. We are very willing to serve persons with disabilities, and others in need. Unfortunately, by not providing reciprocal opportunities for them to serve us, we risk taking away one of their basic needs. We must all, able and disabled, consciously seek ways to offer service to each other.

Inclusion for John created new experiences, new friends, and a wider scope of people for John to communicate with. He literally became more alive, more involved and more animated.

Angelo Bonitatibus
Teacher

In this setting the peers are a powerful model as well as a tool and we are challenged to make sure that we take full advantage.

Meg Petkoff
Supervisor, Speech-Language
and Hearing Services

To Belong, to be Accepted, to be Affirmed, to have Success,

to be Challenged to Excellence, to offer Service;

these are our basic needs.

Their presence in our lives tells us that we are loved.

The importance of the child's self-esteem

Teachers know that the image a child has of him/herself affects their learning. A positive self-image is a guarantee of growth, a negative image the reverse. The image we have of ourselves is a reflection of what others think of us. When others see us as happy and outgoing, this mirrors our perception of self. The closer the others are to us, the greater the reflecting.

The significant others in the lives of pupils, able and disabled alike, are parents, family members, teachers, principals, and other students. Their influence goes beyond simply reflecting, to shaping the child's self-image. Pupils, teachers and other school personnel must be aware of their power to influence this process. As parents and educators we know that praise is a greater motivator than blame. Yet we often dilute the experience or effects of success by diminishing it. An outstanding report card is frequently greeted not by "Well done", but by "You could have done better". Those who were told by a well-meaning music teacher, "Just mouth it, don't sing", frequently gave up on music altogether. We should never underestimate the impact of what we say on the child's developing self-image.

Small children who see themselves as smart, who believe that their mummies and daddies and teachers think they are smart, acquire skills and knowledge with ease. They *are* smart.

I find it reassuring that almost 100% of early childhood and kindergarten pupils believe they are smart and their teachers and parents believe it too. Unfortunately the percentage of believers drops as we go up the grades. What are we doing in our multi-million dollar institutions that cause young children, who entered school confident in their ability and worth, to become doubters? We must support teachers in what they do best; to nurture the learning of each child, nourish their feelings of self-worth, and educate the whole child.

Mark - behaviour concerns, depression, social problems. Mark's self-esteem has gone through the roof this year.

Alex DeStephanis
Special Education Resource Teacher

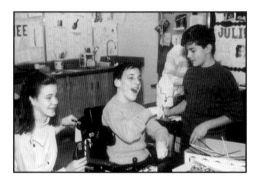

In a climate of support and inclusion special students certainly flourished.

Vincenza Travale
Superintendent

The importance of positive socialization

Socialization is less understood as a core function of the school. Socialization itself is not well understood. Socialization is not just about learning how to get along at a party, although teenagers remind me that is important. It begins at birth and cannot be stopped. It cannot be separated from other functions. It occurs in the home, at school, everywhere, willed or not. It is ongoing. It can be influenced. It can be directed. It cannot be stopped. Opportunities for learning and acquiring social awareness, understanding and skills are important for every child; they are crucial for a child with a disability. Our social interactions and relationships are based on this growing knowledge of self and awareness of others.

Children, in their early years, mimic their parents' words, speech patterns, and actions. They begin to understand rules, roles and expectations. Because they do not always follow the rules, they experience consequences. As they grow, children become more aware of the need for discipline and good order in their lives. Social experiences, which have their heart in the family, are the means through which we develop our personal and social values.

What if something goes wrong, and we fail to make the connections between our needs, wants and appropriate social actions? Socialization need not and should not be left simply to chance. If not caught, it can certainly be taught. Parents, peers and teachers, by word and example, help children obtain and maintain the good will and good opinion of others.

Some children, because of their disability, may be judged as unattractive by those with little experience interacting with them. However unfortunate or unfair this may be, it is a reality. An inclusive education provides opportunities for the sort of day-to-day relationships that help us see beyond the physical limitations and to make genuine personal contact with the other person. Young children are particularly adept at ignoring physical differences in others.

It is also true that we can influence the extent to which we are accepted in the community.

I have been amazed at the positive influence the "chosen" children have on the others. I have been overwhelmed at the kindness and sincerity of other classmates no matter what age.

Joanna Gatto-Adams
Teacher

They are having a typical experience; they are behaving like typical teenagers; they belong.

Jan Burke-Gaffney
Parent

The way we dress, take care of our appearance and communicate, our sense of humour and social skills, all these affect the impression we make on others. All are acquired skills and can be learned, often by modelling the behaviour of others, or through our interactions with friends and family. If a child with a disability is to grow and be accepted in society, he/she must hone these and other social skills. Able or disabled, if your manner of eating is disgusting to others, if you don't smell nice, if you dress "funny", if you act strangely, you will not be accepted.

In the early stages of our inclusive journey in Hamilton, it was not uncommon to welcome students with disabilities from other boards. Many arrived with behaviours that were inappropriate, unpleasant, unacceptable and crude. These were learned behaviours. The children were socialized to act as they did. And socialization cannot be turned on and off like a light switch. We may judge the fruits of socialization to be good or bad, acceptable or unacceptable, but we cannot stop socialization. We can't pretend to teach children at school and leave the socialization to you at home.

Older students can generally change socially unacceptable behaviour by watching others. A young man who transferred into high school took all his clothes off when he went to the washroom. He stopped this strange and time-consuming behaviour abruptly because of the words and example of his classmates.

Another example, a sixteen-year-old boy, a wheelchair user, came directly from a "school for the retarded". It soon became apparent that he was capable academically. He had many social skills. His sense of humour and typical adolescent behaviour made him popular in the school. He soon learned that his disability did not give him immunity from school rules, nor shelter him from the consequences of breaking the rules. His inclusion in a regular high school was complete. His department head suggested privately and tactfully that he should shave regularly and give more attention to hygiene. The advice was accepted with good grace but

He emanated a rather unpleasant odour and drooled profusely. I describe him this way not because I was taken by his arrogance, but because his intellect did not fit his appearance. I discovered him to be bright, perhaps even gifted in many areas.

Tony DeMarco
Special Education Resource Teacher

Many classmates benefited from their presence - they have learned humility, compassion, caring, and understanding.

John Shkopiak
Teacher

generally ignored. One day all of this changed. The beard was gone, the clothing was changed, and the scent of after-shave lingered in the air. "How come?", asked the department head. The young man's answer clearly indicated the power of socialization to change behaviour. "Sir, there are *chicks* you know". It was interesting that his "involuntary drooling reflex" did not function in the presence of girls. The teenage years provide a peer master class in "cool".

Parents have a responsibility to help children with disabilities to be accepted. It may be one of the great injustices of life, however, that children who are "cute" get a better deal than those who are not. Dress your child appropriately, help take care of his/her personal needs, insist on good manners and age-appropriate behaviour, all at the level appropriate to the ability of the child.

Our experiences of socialization, in the family, school and community, provide us with the rules and norms of social behaviour and interaction. The skills we learn through socialization enable each of us to live our lives productively in harmony with others. It is wrong to restrict, by our placement decisions, these educational and social experiences for our children and adolescents. How can one learn "normal", if never exposed to it?

The inability to achieve academically must not deprive any child from the benefits of full and positive socialization in schools and community.

Inclusion does work; it is a God-given right and it is the way of accepting each and every one of us in all of our wonderful perfection and imperfection.

Christine (Bunny) Sawyer
Teacher

Chapter 5
"Why Hamilton? Why 1969?

The seeds of change

I should make it clear from the outset that we did not invent nor even pioneer inclusion in schools. There are many examples in our own Board, across Ontario and elsewhere, of pupils with disabilities being accepted into regular mainstream schools and regular classes.

Although inclusion was not usual before 1969, it was not unknown. In 1961, Lina Verbickas, a grade one teacher at Blessed Sacrament School accepted a young boy with Down Syndrome into her class of 52 pupils. Many teachers had been modifying their teaching and programmes to meet the diverse needs of their pupils. They recognized that no two children had similar needs or abilities and were prepared to teach to those individual differences. Where present, however, such initiatives depended on willingness and individual commitment. Inclusion was the exception, not the rule.

My first experience with inclusion goes back to 1968 at Canadian Martyrs School when we had inclusion and didn't know it.

Frank Goodman
Principal

Pupils with disabilities and the Catholic School system

As already described, the Catholic school system included few pupils with visible disabilities and none with profound disabilities. The curriculum was relatively uncomplicated and the range of subjects offered in the province, even in secondary schools, was not great. The 3 Rs still formed the basis of the Hamilton school curriculum in the mid nineteen-sixties.

Reading was mostly oral. Children read out loud daily, some with ease, others in terror. Writing included a great emphasis on penmanship. A beautiful flowing cursive "hand" was much valued. "Creative" writing was more "formal" than creative, while form including spelling, was frequently more important than content. Arithmetic did not present the challenge that mathematics does today. The emphasis was on rote learning times tables, practising mental arithmetic and solving arithmetic problems.

Neither my penmanship nor my ability to spell correctly marked me out as a scholar and in earlier times, I would probably have been "referred". Fortunately for me, at that time, there would have been no one to receive or deal with the referral.

However, the days of the narrow, formal, lock-step curriculum were numbered. There was an impatience to translate the new wave of educational thinking into reality; to explore non-graded schools, schools without failure and child centred education.

As a young teacher during the late 60's, who had been schooled in the old, rigid, graded, lock-step system prevailing at the time, I was quite satisfied to continue that type of instruction as I began my career.

Lorne Funnel
Principal

Pupils with disabilities and the public school system

The public school system, particularly in the urban areas, had developed extensive, expensive, segregated services for pupils with disabilities. Committed to their traditional approach to serving pupils with special needs, they did not heed the growing volume of demand for change enunciated in the professional literature of the 1960's.

Impact of social change on the development of schools

Hamilton-Wentworth shared with the rest of the province, and indeed the country, a period of tremendous growth, which, as we have seen, required not only new schools, but also more teachers, a precious commodity in short supply across the country. It was at this time, in 1965, that I was appointed principal to the Hamilton Catholic school board.

Hamilton was viewed as a leader in Catholic Education. Elementary schools were governed by a Board of Trustees that was interested, involved and supportive of excellence in the schools.

It was also very open to change and innovation. Over the years a number of our Trustees helped influence the direction of Catholic Education at the provincial level. Dr. N. Mancini was the most notable of these.

In those days in Hamilton, principals and teachers worked in an atmosphere free from undue external supervision. Each school was encouraged to develop its own character. Two Provincial Inspectors of schools served the Hamilton Board. Their duty was to ensure that the acts and regulations were followed. They carried out annual classroom visits. Although the presence of the Inspector in the school caused some anxiety, they in fact offered encouragement and affirmed the work of the teachers. Frank Cunningham and Bill McRae did much to support growth and change.

Role of principals

When the Provincial Inspectors were subsequently withdrawn, the principal, of necessity, assumed a stronger leadership role in his/her school. The period of time without inspectors or supervisory officers was, in my opinion, the period of greatest growth in the schools.

Peter Burns and I were principals in Hamilton during this period of "freedom" from supervisors. Our challenge upon becoming Supervisory Officers was to maintain the atmosphere of personal responsibility while providing opportunities for interaction and necessary system standards and practices.

Continuing shortage of teachers

However, the teacher shortage of the 1960's was still proving difficult to solve. Traditionally, teachers had been trained in "Normal Schools", later called Teachers Colleges.

Twenty-seven years ago I arrived in Hamilton with very rigid and school-centred, as opposed to child-centred, concepts of what good education should be.

Tom Stoneburgh
Principal

Those who successfully completed a prescribed number of subjects in Grade 13 were permitted to seek admission to a Teachers College. In those days, students generally left Teachers College at the age of twenty or younger.

When it became clear that existing training programmes were still insufficient to meet the demands of the 1950's and 1960's, a special programme was established. Graduates of Grade 12 were permitted to teach after successfully completing a six-week summer teacher-training course. These teachers in later years, referred to themselves as the "six week wonders".

Hamilton Catholic Board schools were fortunate to have retained a fairly large group of Sisters of various orders, teaching and giving leadership in the schools. The secular staff was mostly women. In 1960 there were fewer than twenty-five men teachers in the Elementary Schools of the Board.

As we have seen, the nature of society in Hamilton continued to change, and to change rapidly. Jobs were plentiful, and for most people, wages were sufficient to allow them to buy a home, raise a family and live in peace.

When we started, none of us knew what the end would be.

Betty Browne
Superintendent of Student Services

Diversity: The energizing effect of teacher recruitment from abroad

Despite the home-grown solutions described above, the colleges remained unable to supply the quantity of qualified teachers needed in Ontario schools, nor were the unqualified persons hired by the Boards suitable to meet the needs of the schools and pupils. As a result, Hamilton embarked on an ambitious teacher recruitment campaign. This proved highly successful and the Board welcomed the energizing influx of teachers from other provinces and countries. England, Ireland, Scotland and Wales sent the greatest number. Many teachers subsequently came to us from the Caribbean and some from the United States of America. All of these helped us solve our immediate problem and added to the diversity of our communities.

These new teachers enriched the culture of the Board, bringing with them ideas and practices that were new to us. They also brought a desire to learn from and to share ideas with us. In this heady climate, educational and social change was inevitable. Their diverse backgrounds, energy, determination and skills added extra dimensions and variety to the existing cultures within our schools. Most of these new teachers were mothers and fathers with young families. They believed that this country and this community had something to offer them. They certainly had something to offer us.

The teachers who joined us, recruited and home grown, young and ambitious, looked to a long happy vocation, while others nourished dreams of promotion within the Board. All were hungry for professional development through formal courses, in-service training or any other means.

I had the honour of being a greeting committee of one for many of the teachers who came to this Board from other lands. It was a privilege to watch them grow and become leaders in the schools. We would have been less without them.

Our schools were Catholic and Parish centred. Our school community had become a melting pot of languages, cultures, customs, needs and expectations. Respect for difference and acceptance of others was not only a duty, but also a necessity for growth and survival. This was the setting and the atmosphere that would foster "Each Belongs". Teachers and principals who each day encountered and accepted, without question, diverse tongues,

When I returned to Scotland I had been persuaded of the basic positions of integrationists that you make children more normal by placing them in normal settings and that normality will maximize opportunities for children with every type of disability.

Robbie Thompson
Exchange Teacher

customs that were unfamiliar, and a wide range of academic needs, were unlikely to be disturbed by the presence of children with disabilities.

Creating the leaders

Teachers were honored by the parents and trusted by the Board. Many of us embarked on graduate studies in Education. Our schools became alive with new methods and curricula. We welcomed in-service and the great opportunities for leadership, formal and informal.

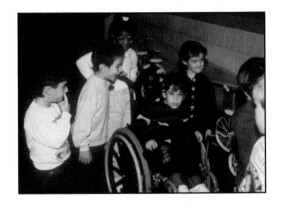

Part of this new dynamic was generated by the Ontario Institute for Studies in Education (OISE) based in Toronto, a relatively easy car drive from Hamilton. OISE had already developed an international and burgeoning reputation for research and teaching, attracting staff and students worldwide. Many teachers in the Hamilton Catholic system, leaders and potential leaders in the Board, enrolled. Much was learned in the formal structure of the university. But it was a tough call whether the most volatile seminars took place on the university campus, or in the weekly car pool from Hamilton to Toronto.

The imperative for educational change inevitably challenged existing values and practices in respect of special needs. Those who were advocating child-centred education insisted that the benefits should be available for all pupils - including those with disabilities. The heady mix of a demand for change, visionary leadership, and supportive trustees inexorably led to new understandings and a redefinition of education; a definition which demanded that "Each Belongs". Although shaken from time to time, that commitment clearly remains central to the basic fabric of the Board.

In nineteen sixty-eight we also witnessed a major re-organization of Ontario's administrative educational structures. The provincial government amalgamated school boards into larger organizational units. The Hamilton Roman Catholic Separate School Board (H.R.C.S.S.B.) and the separate school boards from the communities of Dundas, Stoney Creek, Waterdown, Elfrida and Freelton joined together to form the H.W.R.C.S.S.B. The newly formed Board hired its own supervisory officers to administer the schools and advise the trustees on educational policy, a role previously held by provincially appointed school inspectors.

The process of amalgamation and the introduction of in-house supervisory officers was not without pain or controversy and a history of the introduction and growth of the Board would make compelling reading.

Patrick (P.J.) Brennan, a man of broad experience and wisdom, was appointed Superintendent of Education (the title was later changed to Director of Education). Peter Burns and myself, both of us experienced local principals, were appointed Assistant Superintendents of Education. Senior support staff consisting of Tom Meyers, Jim Sherlock, Tom Mahoney and Steve Simon completed the senior administration of the Board.

In addition to my duties as School Inspector (as my post was then named), I was also assigned responsibilities for special education. I was happy to assume that duty. Let it be known, that at the time, I had no clear vision or blueprint of what it would come to be! It did seem to me that the services provided for students with special needs were restricted to "care and security" rather than education.

It took a year as we assembled the administrative and supervisory team to come to grips with the extent of the needs.

P. J. Brennan
Emertius Director of Education

Influence of Hamilton School Board on educational thinking and developments

Happily, I discovered that many persons in the Hamilton Separate School Board shared my interests, insights and beliefs. Each of those who were part of the 1969 Report, and others who joined along the way, were responsible for the development of a culture of Inclusion.

"Each Belongs" became far more than a mere slogan.

Patrick Brennan's appointment indicated the direction the Board would follow. He was not only open to change, he encouraged it. Special education and secondary education were both targeted for review, with full backing of the Board's trustees. Their approval gave legitimacy not only to the process, but also to its conclusions and directions. These women and men had no idea, at the time, that their approval would create a climate of respect for, and acceptance of, each child as a valued member of their school community. They took the first step to a productive education for children with special needs. They should be proud.

The planning and implementation of the Special Education Review, recommended by the Superintendent of Education and approved by the Board, became my task. I was happy to accept this responsibility and was determined to include as many people as possible in the process.

What were my views of special needs and programmes?

My educational philosophy had been honed by my own teaching experiences and role as a school principal. Yet there remained as many questions as answers.

Questions as to who was or was not exceptional seemed to depend on so many things that had little to do with the children. For instance, at that time, (and to this day, in some administrations) immigrant children, boys and the poor, were more frequently represented in special education than other groups. Some schools identified significant percentages of pupils as having special needs while others made no such identification for children with much the same characteristics! Students with apparently similar needs were more frequently identified as "exceptional" in Boards that had special programmes than in Boards that did not.

Things that facilitate inclusion:
- *proper funding*
- *getting your staff on board*
- *informed and enthusiastic support staff*
- *plentiful resources*
- *positive and effective professional development*
- *strategies that are regular-teacher friendly*
- *not too labour intensive.*

Gaiyle Connolly
Art and Religion Teacher

Special educational provision seemed to be a refuge for those who could not meet the normal expectations of the school, rather than a place of remediation. The labels used to identify children as exceptional were not helpful. One example is the term "slow learner." This seemed to imply a race. Was fast learning better than slow learning? Was that true for all subject areas? Learning didn't seem to be valued unless it matched the arbitrary, limited expectations of the day.

Nevertheless, I was open to change and happy and lucky to have sufficient authority to work with others to bring about the necessary changes. These changes were to be about the richness and quality of education and services for all our children. And in order to achieve this, we needed to remember that, as administrators, we were also general educators. Alongside our concern for each individual child, in reality, we also had to keep in mind the needs of the majority.

Two significant factors weighed heavily in our favour. First, the Board was not interested in developing alternative or even parallel school systems for children with special needs. Had the Trustees chosen to go in that direction, I would not have involved myself in special education. Secondly, because it is more difficult to change existing programs and practices than it is to follow a new direction, we were fortunate to have relatively few special education programs in place.

The time was ripe for change.

I recall you and your staff making a presentation in Toronto on how special needs children were being served in an integrated setting in Hamilton. I know that this philosophy had an impact on the directions taken by the Metropolitan Separate School Board and many other Boards in Ontario.

Jeffy Ponikvar
Emeritus Director of Education

Chapter 6
Creating our fully inclusive educational system:
"The 1969 Report"

The Ontario Provincial Government's re-organization of its school boards in 1968 inevitably required a review of procedures and practices to integrate the newly amalgamated educational services. The re-organized Hamilton Board quickly recruited a dynamic group of teachers and leaders, attracted by the opportunity to take part in creating a values led, forward looking system of education. That these new appointees and existing staff shared a common concern and commitment to the education of the poor and vulnerable within the school community was a further blessing.

The resultant 1969 Review provided an opportunity to appraise existing practice and create an educational system to match the hopes and aspirations of parents, teachers, principals and administrators. This was to prove a turning point on our road to inclusion.

In the early 1970's special education was badly in need of a complete overhaul in the Hamilton Wentworth Catholic School Board. Children were segregated, funding was poor, morale was low.

*John Grosso
Superintendent, In-Service Training*

"The Special Services Report, 1969"

The design and implementation of the review, its findings and recommendations, served as the template for developing Hamilton's own system of inclusive education. However, the key to change lies not in the specific recommendations but in the process and planning which led to their creation.

Pat Brennan (Director of Education) came to the Board with considerable experience as an educational administrator and inspector. He realized the need for a root and branch review of special education, in sharp contrast to the piecemeal approach of the past. Special education was also chosen for review because of the paucity of available information, and such information as was available seemed incompatible with the direction being taken by mainstream education.

From the start Pat Brennan involved as many Board staff and teachers as possible on the basis that, if they were part of the process, they would have a greater commitment to the outcomes.

Membership of the Planning Group for the 1969 Report.

A Special Services Committee (SSC) was established to carry out the review, with John Kaposy (Principal St Daniel's School) as secretary. John's organizational and logistical skills allowed the members of SCC to complete their task in timely fashion while simultaneously carrying out their regular duties in the school and Board systems. This was to be no "ivory tower" exercise.

We chose the sixteen SSC members from a range of backgrounds to ensure "an intelligent awareness of the needs of each child in the Board's educational system."

Working Guidelines

We adopted the following guidelines for the review:

§   To review the literature and practice in the area of learning disabilities,

§   To identify the number of children within the Board falling within that definition,

§   To review the Board's current provision for those children,

§   To formulate a philosophical and educational framework in which the needs of all children could be met,

§   To identify the staffing requirements to implement the programmes and support the framework,

§   To provide a comprehensive report, and make specific recommendations to the Superintendent of Education.

Educational Background to the Review

The new wave of educational thinking that characterised Hamilton during the late 1960's provided the impetus for reviewing the Board's philosophy and provision in the area of special programmes.

There was general agreement that "in the past, schools for the most part were organized for a group of children rather than placing the emphasis on the individual." Knowledge was divided into packages and given grade designations. Children were admitted to the school according to an age criterion. All children within a given classroom were presented with the same material in the same manner. Tests and exams were frequently administered to determine the degree of assimilation of the materials presented. Promotion or failure were based on the results of these tests. Little provision was made for individual differences within the group. Children with special needs were segregated in special programmes and classrooms. Even here, however, all children within a given category were given the same programme. Stated differently, a label was attached to a particular disability, a remedial programme developed and applied to all children bearing the label.

The SSC highlighted the paradox that "while the growth of many pupils was impaired by one limiting factor or another, there was a lack of clear, valid scientific evidence of the effectiveness of the special programmes being provided".

We resolved this problem by proposing that, in the absence of evidence, "practice needs to

If people are looking for a quick fix, it doesn't happen, so all need to make a long term commitment to make inclusion succeed.
Betty Browne
Superintendent of Student Services

be justified by the principles and philosophies which guide our thinking." The days of "ad hoc-ery" were over.

Design of the Review

The SSC established five sub-committees, with each group being allocated a separate area of pupil need to review (e.g. services for disadvantaged and exceptional children, guidance services).

The data collection phase took the following form:

- A comprehensive literature review
- Interviews with individuals possessing relevant expertise and or experience
- The collation and analysis of pupil data from within the Board
- An audit of existing services and provision for pupils with special and exceptional needs.

You have to take the lead and take the mystery out of special education.

Steve Travale
Teacher

In addition there were ceaseless rounds of consultations, discussions and debates within the board, with teachers, principals, parents and others.

The whole of this phase was conducted with great rigour. For instance, the literature review was remarkably comprehensive, with over 115 professional journals, reference books, policy documents and international articles being consulted. These wide-ranging sources covered educational, social and psychological research related to teaching and learning, gifted children, learning difficulties, sensory impairment, physical handicap, emotional disturbance and social maladjustment.

The interviews were similarly extensive. Forty-seven "expert witnesses" were contacted, including teachers (general and special), principals of mainstream and special schools, university teaching and research departments (including OISE), Child and Family Centres, Vocational schools, police, counsellors and psychiatrists, psychologists and superintendents from other school boards.

Assistant Superintendents and school Principals audited the existing provision and conducted a documentary and school data survey to determine the number of pupils within the Board who had been identified as "exceptional," or were seen to be experiencing difficulties within school.

Analysis and Formulation

The data analysis revealed that, at the time of the survey, 23,000 pupils were being educated in the Board's schools. Of these pupils, approximately 21% had been identified as having special needs. (Note: This figure was almost identical to the 20% proposed in the later UK Report into Special Educational Needs {'The Warnock Report,'1978}). We found variations between schools in the incidence of pupils identified as having special needs. Percentages were higher in urban (as opposed to rural) and primary (as opposed to secondary) schools.

Analysis of the consultations, discussions and sub-group findings was a complex task and the time spent by the SSC in clarifying our initial values, ideology and purposes paid rich dividends.

Evidence of the unsatisfactory nature of special education at the time was cited in the Hall-Dennis Report (1968), which described the "inflexible programmes, out-dated curricula, unrealistic regulations, regimented organization and mistaken aims" prevalent in Ontario at the time.

A review paper by Dunne (1967) also challenged the continued existence of special

The work of these teachers should be recognized by establishing sound programming supports and sound objective management procedures.

Dr. Dan Allan
Teacher of Gifted Education

classes; "I have loyally supported and promoted special classes for the educable mentally retarded for the last 20 years, but with growing disaffection. In my view, much of the past and present practices are morally and educationally wrong. We have been living at the mercy of general educators who have referred their problem children to us. And we have been generally ill-prepared and ineffective in educating these children."

We were strongly critical of the Board's own assessment procedures, which were largely confined to intelligence testing: "This type of evaluation generally succeeds in telling us what we already know." We advocated a fresh approach to assessment, one which would *diagnose* the difficulties and *prescribe* the curriculum to help the child overcome them. This assessment would take place within the child's own school by his/her teachers as part of the regular teaching arrangements; "Disability labelling would then disappear, to be replaced by descriptions of the educational curricula and appropriate methods of teaching and learning."

A great deal of our analysis focused on disability and special needs issues. However the break with the past was signalled by the Report's emphasis on child development and the premise that every child's learning should be located within a common educational framework.

The aim to provide "education for all," while simultaneously respecting individual differences and needs, resulted in a model of "special education" which underpinned the Report's values, findings and recommendations. If each child is respected, unique and exceptional, schools need make no distinction between "special" and "normal". Meeting each pupil's special or individual needs becomes the normal thing for schools and teachers to do.

Students were able to progress at their own speed.

Paul Blake
Superintendent

Every child will be looked upon as a dynamic, growing human person, one who has not been labelled and one whose problems will not necessarily limit his/her future possibilities for growth.

A good education, therefore, supports the learning, rights, aspirations and dignity of each learner. Supported by research evidence and philosophical principles, the SSC thereby proposed a simple, coherent framework for the education of all children, including those with significant individual needs, within the mainstream setting.

The expectation that children with special needs would be true, equal members of the school community and that special education and general education would become one, required, in the jargon of the time, one enormous paradigm shift.

We adapted, we changed the physical layout of classrooms to accommodate those with hearing aids, those with white canes, we grouped differently to maximize the strength of our students.

Bill & Sue Nelan
Teachers

Principles:

Our analysis led to the formulation of the following six principles to underpin future planning and practice within the Board's educational arrangements.

1. The function of education, in general, is to provide opportunities for each individual to develop his/her "unique nature – to become most fully what she/he is."

2. The function of education provided in school is to assist, to encourage and to provide opportunities for each child and young person to develop his/her unique combination of skills, talents, abilities and interests. To develop awareness of him/herself and of others, of the communities, group societies, and world in which the person lives and to develop reasonable values. Education in school will always be characterised by a tension between our belief in encouraging children to develop in their own way and our belief that we know, through greater experience, what is the best means of helping them to do so.

3. The function of education is to provide for the needs of each child in an individual way. Schools must devise appropriate organizational arrangements, curricula, teaching techniques and attitudes.

4. School systems must assume a major responsibility for the logical, calculated, systematic development of appropriate means by which these ends may be achieved.

5. All children should be considered as "exceptional" in that they are unique individuals. In this sense, there should not be "special education" for "exceptional children"; rather, there should be available to every child those educational provisions which are designed to meet his/her particular needs.

6. Integration of all children into the ordinary school system is a reasonable aim. It does not require a revolutionary re-thinking of current attitudes, or the practices and provisions based on them.

Look around at the many teachers, teacher assistants, principals, superintendents, and staff who have given so much of their energy, life and commitment to building a caring, inclusive and happy system.

Pat Brennan
Emeritus Director of Education

Despite that final disclaimer, and with the advantage of hindsight, we were clearly moving into unexplored territory. That we maintained our sense of purpose and direction is perhaps attributable to the fact that it was driven by practitioners, grounded in their day to day practice of trying to achieve "a good education" for all the children within their care.

Review of Recommendations

The Report produced 21 recommendations of which 12 were listed as priorities. The following section outlines the main points and highlights some of the principles and values on which the recommendations were based.

Recommendation 1

Significantly, the first recommendation focused on child assessment and programme design. The Report proposed a "diagnostic and prescriptive approach" which would introduce child centred principles into the area of pupil assessment. Some children, perhaps all children, have limiting factors. The key questions to be asked by teachers are: *"Who is John? What are his needs? What is his background and experience? What interventions appear helpful?"* This is the basis of the diagnostic prescriptive approach to teaching and learning for each child. It can be elaborated by teacher profiling of the child's individual strengths, interests, educational difficulties and gifts, all of which would serve as the basis for designing the pupil's individual learning programme.

I realized the following truths; withdrawing children for remediation should be very short term, and in-school special education resource people should spend as much time in the classroom as in the resource room, especially with older students.

Allan Warden
Teacher

Every child can grow and has the right to expect that those to whom his education is entrusted will be very conscious of his potential and his dignity.

In circumstances where the general teacher encountered difficulties in devising or implementing an individual programme she/he would seek help from the school's instructional assessment team.

> *In the past, failure was pupil failure. Now, failures would be programme and instructional failures.*

This signified the end of intelligence testing within the Board and was a radical step at that time, not only in Hamilton. Some boards and education authorities in Canada, USA, and the UK continue to the present day the practice of describing children in terms of IQs, standard scores and percentiles. Such an approach, totally inconsistent with the Board's child-centred philosophy and respect for the dignity of the learner, was rejected.

> *Every child will be looked upon as a dynamic, growing human person, one who has not been labelled, one whose problems will not necessarily limit his future possibilities for growth.*
>
> *1969 Report*

I think we need to celebrate diversity because I think basic to an inclusive school is a sense of community.

Mary Galarneau
Principal

Recommendation 2

We proposed a teamwork model "whereby the various personnel found within the school will be integrated in their functions." Staff who are themselves teaching in isolated settings, or without support, are not in a position to provide an inclusive education for those they teach. Each school would be allocated one learning resource teacher and a teacher counsellor.

The school's instructional team would now comprise the Principal, a general teacher, the learning resource teacher and, where appropriate, the teacher counsellor. The learning support and guidance teachers would also have a consultancy role with the principal in addition to their membership of the school's assessment/ instructional team. The "teamwork recommendation" was vital in order to deliver the benefits of the supports and services being brought to the child within the normal classroom.

Services needed not only to integrate their own functions, but also to work creatively with the school on extending its own problem solving, assessment and team building skills.

> *The team approach both within the school and at other levels within the educational hierarchy seems to hold much promise for the future.*

My personal involvement began with an 8 year old Down Syndrome student. I later realized he was one of the first such students in the province to be integrated in a regular classroom.

Colm Harty
Teacher

Recommendation 3

The SSC proposed a comprehensive set of central level special services. These included psycho-social, special education and guidance teams, whose function was to support the school's curriculum and assessment teams. The learning resource teacher was allocated a critical role in this process.

In the past, special education teachers who operated in isolated classroom settings were unable to extend influence on the rest of the school … in spite of the fact that, very often, they were among the most knowledgeable persons on the staff in the schools in the area of child development and learning theory.

Recommendations 4, 5, 6

We made a number of specific recommendations describing personnel and role of the Board's central Special Services staff whose function was to provide support to the school-based instructional and assessment teams. The general teacher in the classroom, now supported by the school's instructional team and Board's special services, remained at the heart of the new philosophy.

Recommendations 7 and 15

Additional professional support for teachers included a comprehensive in-service training programme, backed up by a library/resource centre "designed to prepare our professional staff to properly meet the needs of all children under our educational jurisdiction."

Recommendations 8 and 12

With hindsight, recommendations eight and twelve now seem less compatible with our guiding principles. In recommendation eight we proposed a feasibility study to assess the possibility of admitting children to kindergarten on the basis of "readiness." We also proposed that the Board consider the establishment of a Diagnostic Learning Centre.

We believe that what children are and become is in great part a reflection of what teachers and significant persons in their life believe about them.

Other points of note included pre-kindergarten ("Head-Start") facilities and "compensatory education programmes" for culturally or socially disadvantaged children.

Perhaps our major achievement was not to be found in the specific recommendations, but in the shift of philosophy, focus and language. Our philosophy was unapologetically of education, not special education. We focused on the child as the learner, on the individual and his/her unique gifts and differences, rather than on the group or the class and their given category and shared programme. Teachers, henceforth, were to be working as part of a staff team rather than in a segregated class setting.

> *Special education should be viewed as an integral part of the regular school programme.*

By all these means, the neighbourhood school, supported by the appropriate level of staff expertise, supports and resources, was now able to welcome each child within its catchment area. Each child would belong. The days when parents whose children had significant needs were required to seek help and schooling from neighbouring jurisdictions were at an end.

> *Because our school system espouses a philosophy that is quite distinct and unique … it was felt that the needs of the total student population would be met more adequately. Because of this, Special Education, per se, should not exist as a separate, isolated educational function.*

Our final recommendation was that SSC "should be allowed to continue its operations as an officially appointed body". The Board was in for the long haul.

There was to be no turning back.

Chapter 7

Delivering the Promise

The shelves of our school boards, local education authorities and schools are heavy with the weight of well-intentioned documents whose worthy aims never quite came to fruition. That was not the fate of the 1969 Report.

This section summerises the impact of the Report, and how specific recommendations were translated into practice within the Board and its schools. It had an impact and became the road map to inclusion.

Recommendation One, the diagnostic-prescriptive approach to assessment, was adopted immediately and continues today. It was linked to the role of the special education resource teacher – unfortunately the preferred title of learning resource teacher had already been acquired by the librarians. Eventually every school received its own learning resource teacher (special education). For a period of time, some had two or even three. It was found, however, that the presence of more than one in-house special education resource teacher led to solutions by specialists rather than by the school instructional team. Actual practice now is to have one such teacher per school (0.5 in smaller schools). Teacher counsellors never took hold in the elementary schools but continue at the secondary level.

The concept of a "team approach" was approved and implemented. This gave rise to a genuinely creative innovation; the diagnostic prescriptive team. This team was school based and mandated to meet weekly. It responded to the needs and requests for the students in the school. It helped *prescribe* activities and strategies to *solve* the problems presented. The in-school diagnostic-prescriptive team was also able to draw on additional expertise from

The Board of Trustees bought into the movement toward integration and supported it from the start, when revenues for Catholic Boards were unequal, and never flinched in support of these students no matter how difficult the financial situation for the Board.

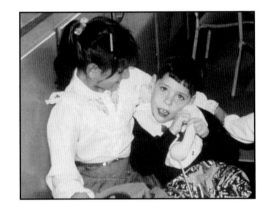

In-service was provided for teachers on Professional Advancement Days during and after school, and on an ongoing basis by Student Services staff.

John Grosso
Principal

the student services team at the central office. This "Hamilton initiative" has been adopted enthusiastically in other school boards.

As indicated above, recommendations three, four, five and six related to the personnel, roles and functions of the Student Services. Student Services was a multi-professional team approach to supporting teachers confronted with planning for a child with highly exceptional or challenging needs. And multi-professional it was. No individual professional had the authority to offer recommendations unilaterally, without the approval of the team. A unique feature was that the school retained and still retains to this day, the power to accept or reject the recommendations.

While most of the remaining recommendations, largely relating to support and developmental activities for pupils and teachers, were and continue to be adopted, there were two significant exceptions. Recommendation eight, the possibility of admitting some children early to kindergarten on the basis of "readiness", introduced the possibility of children being excluded from school. It was, happily, dropped. As was recommendation twelve, the creation of a Diagnostic Centre. Apart from any other grounds, this proposal was philosophically inconsistent with the Board's principle of bringing the supports to the child in the school, rather than taking the child out to the supports.

The 1969 Report did not lie mouldering on some office shelf. It continues to provide inspiration to teachers and breathe life into the Board's philosophy of providing a good education for each child.

I fondly recall these weekly sessions, which to many outsiders seemed a complete waste of time. Yet, to us they were essential to develop a common vision so that we could go after common goals with the best outcomes.

Eugene Perabo
Co-ordinator Central Services
Special Education

Inclusion not only meant all children, but all disciplines too, working together for the child.

Des Brennan
Emeritus Director of Education

Each child has a right to a good and complete education.

Reflections on the 1969 Report

The specific conclusion and recommendations of The 1969 Report were not preordained. However, the mandate provided by the Board in endorsing P.J. Brennan's proposal to review services for pupils with special needs in the educational climate of the time, gave credence to the philosophy and the path that would be followed.

The expectation that children with special needs would be true and equal members of the school community and that special and general education would be one, required, in the jargon of the day, one enormous paradigm shift.

Despite our awareness of the educational literature of the time, we did not fully appreciate our role as change agents. As we saw it, our task was to accept each child, able and disabled alike, and provide them with as good and as complete an education as their needs and our skills allowed. The "path" that we followed in fulfilling this task did lead ultimately to enrolling any child seeking admission to our schools.

The path to a desired end is chosen by those who seek that end; the destination is more important than the path chosen. In everyday living the path is frequently as compelling as the destination. In our context, however, the destination was the sole purpose of the journey.

Looking back from thirty years of inclusion, some see the committee members as visionary and their work as original and innovative. These generous expressions of approval are pleasant and affirming. The reality is that our aspirations were generally simple. Learning was not a race. Learning was to be valued, however acquired, early or late, slow or fast. Together we wished to recommend practices that would develop child centred learning. We knew that child

The most outstanding feature of the Board's policy was the administration's utter certainty that this was the best service for the students and that it could and would be done.

Janet Charlton
Speech & Language Therapist

centred learning would have to include all children, able and disabled alike.

We did not speak of "inclusion." We spoke of mainstreaming and integration, the term "inclusion" being unknown at the time. We did not then rule out some segregated settings, although they were always temporary with specified time limits. Additionally we knew that some children with severe disabilities were not yet officially available to us.

With hindsight, the major contribution of the committee was not only in the detail of programmes and functions; it was in the philosophical underpinnings of what we meant by a "good education for all." John Kaposy, the secretary of the committee, provided the scholarly review of the education literature concerning child centred learning, mainstreaming and integration. His research provided professional legitimacy to the 1969 report. The clear expectation that each person has equal value in the community and that resources, both human and material, would be shared equally by each was the defining moment in the journey to "Each Belongs."

As I write, in 2005, the present negative climate in education both at home and abroad is not justified by these scholarly sources, writings and conclusions.

The promise we made to you as parents was simple. Each child will be enrolled in their neighbourhood school. They will be placed in an age appropriate group. They will receive instruction appropriate to their level of ability. They will be challenged and stretched. If for any reason they are removed from the school, it will be done by proper, due process. They may always return. We will never give up on your child.

Many parents uprooted their families and came to Hamilton because of that promise. Our inability to always meet your expectations, the lure of other options for your child, the weariness that comes from seemingly endless advocacies do not justify the segregation of

There must be obvious commitment to child welfare in the administrative and political committees.

Colm Hardy
Special Education Teacher

Inclusion has come a long way. I entered the profession with one idea. I left with a far different idea. All students belong in the neighbourhood school, and they will be accommodated in our schools.

Lorne Funnel
Principal

In Hamilton, parents no longer have to fight for what is rightfully theirs.

G. Ferguson
Principal

your child. Inclusion is not like a car; it doesn't 'work or not work.' IT IS. Neither parents nor school administration need be perfect to be loved, honoured, and respected. That is a lesson your children have taught us.

Society benefits when each of its citizens, able and disabled alike, are educated. Free societies must ensure that each person receives the education that is suited to his/her needs. If the education of those who have disabilities is not to be seen as an add-on or a work of charity, it must be integrated into the policies of general education and be inclusive of all.

The Report's final legacy was its recognition of the dignity and worth of each individual and his/her right to growth. Its simplicity was the promise that a good, complete education for each pupil, including those with special needs, was a reasonable expectation. The '69 Report has weathered the test of time. Parents and educators tempted to maintain or return to segregated or treatment-based schooling would do well to re-read and ponder its wisdom.

"Each person is endowed with the dignity of a person. Each person has equal value despite differences in ability. Each person has a right to grow and indeed each person can grow. The limits of individual growth are unknown and should not be circumscribed. No person is static, each is ever in the process of becoming. Each person is unique and irrepeatable. The beliefs we hold about people can serve as prison walls limiting us at every turn. They can also set us free from our shackles to confront great new possibilities never dreamed of before. Life is the ultimate gift and learning is its crowning."

No verbal.
Not toilet trained yet.
It seemed like I was admitting a baby.
The medical people said she may not live past puberty.

To my utter astonishment, her life in school took on a new meaning. Her motivation sky-rocketed and progress was back on track.

Eugene Mazur
Principal

Leadership & Commitment to Cathedral High School earned Daniel Paveo the **Jim Hansen Award**

D14 / The Hamilton Spectator

Saturday, June 21, 200.

FAMILY & KIDS

Local Treasures / *Daniel Pavao*

Cathedral 'cheerleader' receives high honours

By SUZANNE BOURRET
The Hamilton Spectator

Daniel Pavao has had a busy and memorable school year.

The special needs student at Cathedral High School recently received the Jim Hansen Spirit of Community Award. It is presented to elementary and secondary school students who are community builders, who demonstrate a commitment to school activities and student colleagues.

He was one of 10 nominated for the award named for Jim Hansen, a pioneer of inclusive education in Canada.

Three weeks ago, Pavao won the Hamilton City Championship 100 metre ambulatory race.

He now has four track and field medals hanging in a prominent place in his bedroom.

"I was so surprised and I was so happy when I found out I got the Jim Hansen award," says Pavao, 19, who has a work placement at Tim Horton's on Kenilworth Avenue.

The award was presented to him two weeks ago at the Hamilton-Wentworth Catholic District School Board on Mulberry Street.

He was nominated for his leadership abilities and his commitment to school activities by being Cathedral's top cheerleader. He attends most school events and encourages everyone around him. Pavao's nomination described him as "a builder of community by demonstrating through his work placement at Tim Horton's, the level of competence that an individual with special needs can achieve when given the opportunity. His level of independence is truly remarkable."

Pavao says he likes helping other special needs students and taking them to classes. "I like to help. I like being nice to people," he says.

He has served as an altar boy and has helped to sort and pack food and clothing for the needy during Christmas collections at Holy Family Church. He also delivers the Free Press for The Hamilton Spectator.

Pavao, who has Down syndrome, plans to continue his studies at Cathedral and hopes to study photography at Mohawk College.

sbourret@thespec.com or 905-526-3305

CATHIE COWARD, THE HAMILTON SPECTATOR

Leadership and commitment to Cathedral High School have earned Daniel Pavao the Jim Hansen award.

Chapter 8

WALKING THE TALK

The school board

Let it be perfectly clear: publicly funded school boards exist to ensure that children and young people who live within their boundaries receive a good, complete education. And that it is the responsibility of the trustees, on behalf of the parents and within the acts and regulations of the Ministry of Education, to set the policies which guide/direct the Board's actions. Within this context the Director of Education and staff have considerable latitude in shaping the Board's philosophy and actions.

Collectively, the trustees, will support any initiative that they believe makes sense. The 1969 Report on Special Education was such an initiative. It was the path to Each Belongs and was unanimously approved as such by the board.

It started as the *talk*. It became the *task*, for the Director, administrator, teachers and support staff to *walk*. I was lucky enough to be asked to set the journey in motion and guide it on its way.

Getting inclusion right from the start: admissions to school

In Ontario, children who reached their fifth birthday by December 31st were eligible to attend school. In most school boards, though not mandatory, it was also the practice for four and five year olds to attend Early Childhood (ECE) or Kindergarten (Kg) programmes. In Hamilton, while in practice these opportunities already existed for children with disabilities, they were consolidated by the 1969 Report. If you were of the right age and breathing, with

One experience I had with a special kid inspired me to never quit. He was walking down the hall gripping the rail trying to get his braces and I asked him if he wanted me to get them for him. He said he was fine and he'd get them himself. He was very sure of himself and I never knew he had that confidence.

Craig, Grade 7

or without a respirator, you were welcomed in to your local mainstream school. Once in, your needs directed your learning.

Most other boards in the province, Catholic and Public, had, and retain, certain regulations and restrictions regarding the admission of children with disabilities to mainstream schools. Cut out the cost of administering such restrictive procedures, transfer the savings to support the kids in mainstream schools and everybody benefits.

We found that children with disabilities who were to begin their school career in ECE or Kindergarten were no more difficult to serve than similar, non-disabled children. A disability does not define a child, nor are we required to bring about a "cure". Our task is to educate, teach and foster their growth. Living and learning alongside other children, able or disabled, is the essential ingredient for achieving that growth. And the early years were ideal for the beginnings of inclusion.

Priorities in funding exceptional needs

Financial decisions often influence services for exceptional pupils, whose inclusion is seen as costly. Inclusion was seen as more costly than the segregated program. We were determined to include each child even if the cost was greater. However, many aspects of education and schooling "cost more". There are no standard or normal costs, School Boards spend money to achieve their goals. Since these expenditures must remain within the boundaries of their revenue, they will need to set priorities for their expenditures.

As an example, a Separate School system adds to the cost of education in the province, it is valued and therefore funded. French language schools add to the cost of education in the province, they are valued and therefore funded. Within each Board costs vary for services

I have been tutoring Tony for some time. He continues to improve consistently, and is gaining more and more confidence in his own capabilities.

Andrea, Grade 12

What I learned from them is that they don't need someone to boss them around.

Tiziane, Grade 4

provided, small schools cost more than large schools, Secondary schools cost more than elementary schools. Proper administration is a significant cost; schools need to be maintained and cleaned, goods ordered, bills paid. The list of expenditures is almost endless. Money will be allocated according to the priorities set by the Board. Expenditures will clearly reflect the values and priorities of the Board of Trustees. In my opinion, the setting of priorities is the most important aspect of the role of trustees.

The clear duty and priority of the Board is the total education of each child under its care. It follows then that the most significant expenditure in every Board is for teachers. That is as it should be since teachers have a profound influence on society's most precious possessions, our children.

In times of financial plenty it is difficult to discern a Board's values and priorities through its expenditures. It is in times of reduced funding and financial restraint that these values become more apparent. What is kept? What is modified or reduced, what is eliminated?

They need us to be understanding and loving to take each of them as an individual and to overlook what they can't do and focus on what they can. They help us to grow and we help them to grow, a nice arrangement, is it not?

Christine, Grade 7

It does not seem unfair to note that when cuts are necessary, they are made mostly in areas not covered by the collective agreements of the employee groups of the Board. These agreements become a Board's highest priority.

Budget reductions, sometimes drastic, are made in non-mandatory or optional programmes. Librarians, Early childhood and Kindergarten programmes are frequent targets because of reduced funding. They are officially "non-mandatory" programmes and therefore can be reduced or eliminated. However, most educator and parents would not equate "optional" with unnecessary.

Special education programmes are at times treated as an add-on to the regular programmes of the Board, they appear to be placed in the same category as "optional" programmes. In times of financial restraint they are among the first programmes to be reduced. They are not "optional" they are "mandatory", therefore cuts in them should be challenged. The pupils that make use of Special Education programmes and services are required to attend school. They are to be valued as are other pupils. In a civilized and compassionate society they are frequently more valued. In practical terms financial cuts are hurtful to staff and students alike. Cuts to Special education programmes however, in addition to being hurtful, reduce the "life chances" of the pupils served by these programmes.

Children in mandatory programmes are served even in time of severe restraint. For example, Grade four pupils are never left at home because of financial restraints, exceptional pupils frequently are. How can this be? Both are required by law to attend school. Is it possible that one group is "valued" more than the others?

Dedicated funding or funding in "envelopes" is a strategy that has been used to attempt to ensure that funding is spent for the specific purpose targeted. This strategy, though well intended, always fails because it is based on distrust. What does one do when the "envelope" is empty and more needs arise? Those who wish all pupils included in the neighbourhood school will not achieve this goal if they insist on funding by labels and programmes. "Each Belongs" depends on an understanding that each pupil has equal value. It requires that the Board insist that resources are shared equitably. For those who value each child, "Each Belongs" cannot be blocked. It becomes easier, however, to achieve and maintain an inclusive school environment if the local Board controls the expenditure of monies allotted.

We as a Board were not free of fault in allocating money, we did however, reaffirm our belief enunciated clearly in the '69 Report that "Each person has equal value in the community,

We learned that blind people have to concentrate with their ears because they can't see what's happening around them.

Tina, Grade 3

From an intimidated individual back then, I have turned into someone who can make a difference.

Monika, Grade 12

that resources, both human and material would be shared equitably by each". This, the defining moment in our journey to "Each Belongs" remains.

The Good News, the reality, is that inclusion costs considerably less than segregated settings. Reduced expenditures would not be the "purest" of motives for inclusion, however, the reason for starting is not as important as the fact of starting. Truly inclusive schools sustain and maintain themselves. In a truly inclusive school, personnel, programmes and materials are used for the general good.

Some learn slower than others, but they're still the same as us. They help us by teaching us the way they learn.
Steve, Grade 4

Challenges

We neither said nor believed it would be easy. We soon discovered that we needed time, patience and some compromise to deal with the challenges we encountered on the journey. A priority task was to work out what to do about the inherited infrastructures – Opportunity classes, Behaviour classes, Development Centres - that stalled the integration of all pupils.

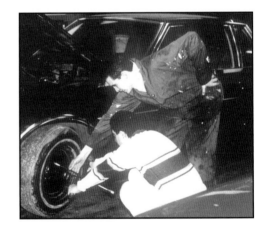

Opportunity classes

In 1969 we had Opportunity Classes for both boys and girls. These were completely segregated entities, and while well intentioned, were totally unacceptable. Their very existence undermined the principles of inclusive education. We managed to eliminate them over time through graduation, amalgamation of classes or inclusion. The pupils who endured these placements should receive an apology.

Behaviour Classes

The most unloved children, mostly boys, whose behaviour presented the most searching challenges to their schools and teachers, were almost always sent to another school or to a behaviour class. In 1969, we not only inherited Behaviour Classes, we also opened a few more. We got it wrong.

What we did learn from this experience, quite early on, was that any improvements achieved in the Behaviour class did not transfer back to the pupil's original host school.

So we recognised the importance of teaching the pupils and addressing their behavioural difficulties in the classroom and / or playground in which they occurred. Removing the child does not help the host school develop its own practices and strategies to deal with these challenges. Nor did the Behavioural classes provide suitable role models from which the pupil can learn.

'Trainable and Educable Retarded' children

'Trainable and educable retarded' was the label attached in the 1950's and 60's to children with significant learning difficulties. Fortunately, its usage has long since been abandoned. The purpose of referring to it here is to point out that children so labelled were then officially under the care of the public Board. As we refrained from using that description, in strictly legal terms we had no such pupils in our Board. Nevertheless, by 1969 we had a fair number of them in our schools.

We preferred to educate, not just label them. With the passage of time parents were permitted to place their child in the Catholic schools, where they belonged and were made welcome. Those who came *lost their label* and *found a place* in age appropriate classes, from Grade 1 to High School.

They can think for themselves. They don't need you to tell them everything.

Lori, Grade 3

The active involvement of people with Down Syndrome in our communities will benefit everyone – as long as this encouraging trend is fostered. As both a parent of a child with Down Syndrome and a primary teacher, I have first hand experience of how meaningful this connection is, both inside and outside of the classroom.

Marie O'Connor (Ireland)

Development Centres

Children with significant learning difficulties were originally placed in 'Development Centres'. The Centres, which were neither schools nor any other form of educational provision, served the most severely disabled children in the Province. At the time it was common practice for psychologists and medical officers to classify some children with severe disabilities as 'uneducable,' and therefore, by some circular logic, incapable of benefiting from education in schools. In Hamilton–Wentworth the provincial Development Centre was located on the site of Our Lady of Lourdes school. This was an interim step in the eventual transfer of jurisdiction of the Centres from the Ministry of Social Services to the Ministry of Education, and hence to our school Board.

The wall of isolation can be broken and this can make such a difference to a person's self confidence and self-image.

Crystal

The Board lobbied hard for the enrolment of these children into a school, and entered into agreements with the Ministries of Education and Social Services to transfer the children from the Centre into the classrooms in the empty wing at Our Lady of Lourdes school. While technically the children may not have been our legal responsibility, they were certainly in one of our schools!

Errol Williams, the principal, immediately included the children into the life and learning of the school. While we did not have a ready-made system of adult support in waiting at the time, we were able to utilise that untapped resource found in all schools – the other pupils. In that way help was soon available and friendships formed. At our request, legal responsibility for the education of the children passed to Our Lady of Lourdes School, and within three years all of these children were transferred to local mainstream schools throughout the Hamilton school system.

The inclusion of these children and students, without any form of labelling, set the standard.

No one need be excluded and not one was excluded. Miracles started to happen! Here are two examples.

Because most of the children were also severely physically disabled and of restricted growth, they were often and mistakenly thought to be no more than eight or ten years old. Therefore they had not been placed in age appropriate teaching groups. On one occasion, two retired principals of the Board, Betty and Mary, came to my office asking what I doing about including the ex Developmental Centre students into age appropriate classes in their High school. When I replied, "We have no space in the High school" they replied "Then where do 15 and 16 year old students go to school in this Board?" I had no answer. They got me.

However, I pointed out my real problem: without room, we couldn't make the provision, without the provision, we couldn't make the move. Again they came back: "What if **we** find the space?" I told them that if they found the space, we had a deal.

Betty and Mary came through. They found a room in St.. Mary's High School that looked like the end of a hall, with a very old fashioned washroom. The latter was immediately designated a 'Retarded Wash Room' by the students, and banned from use in its present state. But with multicoloured painting, murals and all the other things teenagers do, they transformed it into the sort of civilised place they would all wish to use. And inclusion was on its way for those students.

Even washrooms can send out powerful messages about who truly belongs, and who does not.

Another story springs to mind about from that period. One young student, let's call her Lynn, was the classic poster picture of a poor neglected waif. Her head practically touched the ground. She constantly drooled, and made what to us were inappropriate noises. Meg,

I want to show people that we care and we should be friends with everyone.

Michael

the speech pathologist, was determined to help Lynn to develop her language. The Ministry of Education refused the request for funding because it would be a waste of resources, due to what they saw as Lynn's almost total non-capacity to communicate.

Again, we met the self-defeating argument: *"If we believe they can't learn it, why teach it? And so they don't learn it. Which proves we were right. QED."*

We found the money within the Board and the language programme started. Soon, using a concept board and other similar speech and language aids, Lynn was able to start communicating with us. Meg did not believe in the impossible. Nor that efforts to teach a child to learn how to communicate were a waste of time. By the way, the Ministry then began to provide funding for children with similar needs.

Working together helps us to see beyond their disabilities. Our school is a team. We consider them as members of the team.
Kristina, Grade 8

The welcoming of these, the most needy children, was initiated and carried out by the people directly involved. They needed no permission for their ground breaking work. The 'hands off' attitude of the Board certainly left staff free to meet the challenges presented. And regular reports kept the Board informed, and guaranteed their continuing support.

The two stories above illustrate that *when we started our journey to inclusion we hadn't got all the answers. Many of the problems and challenges we only encountered as we went along.* It was by sticking closely to our values and beliefs that we learned how to solve the problems and write the script that became the story of inclusion in Hamilton-Wentworth.

The School Board and its services

If it was the role of the Board to ensure a good, complete education for all children and the job of the Trustees to set policy, it was the superintendents and central support services who provided the most obvious, day-to-day link with practice in schools.

Superintendents and Central Services

The mandate of the 69 Report was clear and directive; the role of the superintendents was to provide support, consultation and encouragement, to schools. They would also visit children with special needs, and, where appropriate, provide access to resources. Their work was not overly prescriptive and staff had some latitude in carrying out the role. In some instances the Board allowed superintendents to modify or change some recommendations, or advise over the timing of their implementation. Examples can be found in preceding chapters. Looking back, actual time lines for implementing the 69 Report's recommendations ranged from instant to as much as 10 years.

The Board's Central Services gradually evolved their identity and philosophy in response to the needs of the schools and the guidance of the Board. Skilled staff were recruited from to develop teaching and curriculum resources. The Services grew from an initial staff of four to more than fifty professionally qualified practitioners, coming from a wide range of disciplines.

As discussed in Chapter 6, the 1969 Report made it clear that the Central or Support Services were to have no authority over the schools or the teachers. Their major trust was the provision of guidance and assistance to the principals and teachers, where needed. This explicit lack of authority was deliberate and the key difference between our own Support

Services and those in other Boards.

· Nor was it the role of Support Service staff to sit in judgment, positively or negatively, on teachers or schools. Where necessary, it was the superintendents who supported the principals in carrying out these tasks.

Schools referred pupils to the Services for assessment and suggestions about curriculum and teaching strategies. Several support staff, from different disciplines, might be engaged in more complex assessments. The final recommendations would have the collective support of each person engaged in the assessment process.

Principals were entitled to accept or reject the recommendations, or to develop their own programmes. But simply doing nothing was not an option.

Were the staff of the support services teachers or clinicians? Many parents and advocates tried to persuade them and the schools to offer a 'treatment service' to pupils. But treatment is not the role of the school. Schools are about education and growth. Children do not attend school to receive treatment during their learning time.

Finally, the Central Support Services also dealt with some longer term and strategic issues, as part of their role to foster learning for all, reaffirming their role as educators, not therapists.

The contribution of visitors to the Board

When a board is seen to offer something "different", people come to see. Since we were seen as "new", we received many such visits. We had to sit down and think. Were these interruptions to our work, or, potentially, could they be seen as a contribution?

Successful Boards and schools are like most other such organizations – they continually need to change, develop and grow if they are to remain successful. Once they lose that motivation and impetus, complacency and decay soon follow. We began to realize that visitors, parents, educators, the curious as well as the sceptical, helped keep us on our toes, and our school system alive and growing. With hindsight, being open to outsiders and their different opinions and values helped Hamilton from becoming stuck or complacent.

At heart, most visitors wanted the answer to two basic questions:

1. Were we serious in our intent to accept and include all children?
2. If so, were we doing it?

They recognized in Hamilton the beginnings of something important, and by visiting and asking questions about what we were doing they became 'unpaid consultants' for our board. Far from a hindrance, they were assisting our journey towards fully inclusive education. We listened to their questions, learned and, where appropriate, we changed as a result of their visits. While they, in turn, had the opportunity for challenge to some of their own preexisting views, values and practice.

A Director of Education from Quebec, left his board and taught for a full month in one of our schools. He wanted to experience Inclusion.

Marsha Forest, an international advocate for inclusion, came from Toronto, with some scepticism, to visit a number of our schools. She saw children, able and disabled alike, learning together. On one occasion, in the early years of the project, we visited together a school containing a class of profoundly physically and intellectually disabled children. She asked me, sharply, "What do you call this class?"

I replied "Terrible! But not for long - it will soon be changed!"

Marsha became a valued colleague and advisor. She believed that there was no magic in beginning inclusion, only adjustments. She changed one school with a single question: "Why do these children have different lockers and home room?" The answer came in the change of location of the home room and random lockers for the children. Her contributions reinforced our belief that the only mandatory requirement for full inclusion was "the other children."

Some external visitors came determined to prove us wrong. Others in the belief that inclusion, in practice, was not possible. They were hard pressed to deny the evidence of their own eyes. Even, or particularly, in these instances, their visits and questions were of value to us. On one occasion the complete Special Education Department of the state of Michigan visited "to see" what we were doing. Impressed by what they saw, and making no public comments, their visit resulted in a profound difference to arrangements for the development of inclusive education for the children of Michigan.

Visitors began to visit our small school board from across the globe, probably seven to ten thousand over the years. We not only enjoyed their visits, they also provided us with great in-service training and opportunities for our own learning. Giving an account of your own practice, and the principles behind it, is a powerful self-learning tool.

The structure of the day was simple and open. Visitors were greeted by a superintendent, but taken on tour by a principal. Any visitor was permitted to enter and visit any of our schools. At the end of the day they sat down for an open discussion with the principal(s) and staff, with no superintendent present. The staff were the 'on the ground' expert practitioners, valued by the visitors and the Board.

Not surprisingly the media began to show interest in what we were doing. They were intrigued by this fresh approach to teaching handicapped children. After initial suspicions they provided positive and accurate coverage of children with disabilities being real students, and not objects of pity, sentimentality or patronage.

I remember being phoned by a reporter from Calgary who asked, "How is your integration working in Hamilton?" I replied with a further question: "How is your Grade Four working in Calgary?" She got the point, and we both enjoyed the humour.

I had numerous invitations to address principals and superintendents from other boards. For example, I ran a session with the principals from Vancouver, who listened and asked questions around making their own highly impressive work more inclusive. They subsequently went on to develop their own "Vancouver solution" to the challenge of creating an educational system where each child truly belongs.

Parents

It may be trite to start this final section with the comment that parents are the first educators, but it is a profound truth. Parents entrust their children to our teachers. However they do not abdicate their overall responsibility and concern for their child.

Parenting any child involves a lot of hard work. While parenting a child with additional or exceptional special needs involves a lot of extra work on top of that. It would not be surprising if some parents, whose child's first educational experience was in a special school, came to value the apparent safety, comfort and simplicity of those arrangements.

Nevertheless, it was our experience that most parents whose children moved from special schools to regular, mainstream programmes soon saw the benefits. They also recognised the valued of 'challenge' for their children. No challenge, no growth.

'Special' normal or normal?

A few parents continued to ask "Where is the (traditional) 'special needs curriculum' of bowling and swimming sessions for our children?" Our consistent answer was "Where ever you take them!" If bowling or swimming is part of the school curriculum for all, that's fine. But 'normal is normal'. You can't have segregation and normalisation. And you can't have separate 'retarded fishing' or bowling.

The job of the school is to provide all children with the appropriate teaching, curriculum and social opportunities for growth, alongside their peers.

On occasion, parents from within our Board asked for a special school placement for their child. This was problematic. We had no such provision. However, we recognised parental rights and parents' crucial role in the education of their child. Either my superintendent colleague, Phil Di Francesco, or I would spend a day with the parent(s) visiting and reviewing the provision we made in our own schools, for all children. Back at the office, at the end of the day, we would discuss with the parent what they were looking for, and what we could provide. Almost invariably they opted in to our system. If not, we would pay for their child to attend that provision in a neighbouring Board.

Advocacy groups

In the early years, parents in the Board formed separate, specific advocacy groups for children with similar disabilities; for instance, children with autism, cerebral palsy or significant learning disabilities. Their purposes were varied. Many focused on fund raising. Others looked for mutual support, while most lobbied for additional staff and resources to be provided for their named group. This fragmentation tended to exaggerate the isolation, rather than support community and network building, as each group acted for its own purposes and clients.

We were not prepared to segregate our pupils, nor were we prepared to support advocacy groups that were separated by label. How far would such fragmentation go? We might end up one day with an advocate group for every part of the body!

We responded to these movements by addressing the needs that underpinned their creation and worked together to establish a group called "Parents of pupils with special needs. " The group met monthly with Board staff, including myself, present as visitors. But the ownership and development of the group was parent led and managed.

Within that setting they advocated for each other. And with that generic name all parents could be included. It was a privilege and pleasure to learn from the involvement of parents of the gifted, the physically disabled, children with terminal conditions, and others, and to experience the focus on the common goal of a good education for each child.

The Promise

Parents in our schools are given a simple promise. To this day we have kept that promise. Your child, able or disabled, is welcome and will be a full participant in his or her school and class. Your child will never be removed permanently. In the event of any short-term removal, for whatever reason, due process will be followed. And your child remains welcome to return. Always.

What have we learned about developing inclusive education?
Comments from Hamilton School Board

1. There is not any one ideal setting or one right way to do it.

2. No child can fail inclusion.

3. There are no prerequisite skills or behaviours that are necessary before a child can be successfully included.

4. Teachers do not need special training to be successful in inclusive classrooms.

5. Inclusion is most likely to be seen as successful by those involved when a co-ordinated, supportive team approach is used.

6. Teachers and children should not be afraid to make mistakes and to learn from them.

7. Take things one day at a time. Don't try to solve all the problems today or even this week!

8. An Individualized Education Plan, with clear goals and rationales, that has had plenty of input from everyone, including parents, goes a long way towards feeling like "we're on the right track and progress is being made."

9. This is a journey where we all are learning, step by step, as we travel. Be patient with ourselves and one another!

10. Even if it feels like everything is going wrong, keep at it, talk with others, ask for help … some days are like that. Remember, this is real life.

With acknowledgements to
Betty Browne,
Phil Difrancesco
Mary Galarneau
Jackie Bajus

IN MEDIA RES

The stirring of the status quo created the climate for the tremendous achievements we've had in extending service to all our children, and particularly to those children with disabilities.

P. J. Brennan, Emeritus Director of Education

"And particularly to those children with disabilities". With these words we close for now the story of the journey toward inclusion for all of Hamilton-Wentworth Catholic District School Board (HWCDSB). But the story is not ended. We close in media res, in the middle of the action. The Board and its people continue the story, working to serve all its learners, no matter what differences of colour, language, ethnic origin, or ability they might have. The people of HWCDSB understand that inclusion involves every learner.

Pat Brennan, the senior administrator of HWCDSB at the beginning of the Board's journey to inclusion, chose well when he handed responsibility for including all learners to Jim Hansen, and those who worked with him. The Board has chosen well since as responsibility for the initiative has changed hands: Phil DiFrancesco, Betty Browne, Jackie Bajus, every teacher and every principal. All have shared the vision of a truly inclusive system. All have carried the vision forward as it has expanded to include every learner without exception, making every teacher a daily leader in educational innovation. Daily they are marking paths for others to follow through the wilderness of special education, segregation, and educational inequity.

Even as we close the story for now, we are sharply aware of the need for communicating the vision and its reality. HWCDSB began its change long ago. Other innovative school systems across Canada and beyond have created their own paths. However, most school systems remain in that wilderness, either unaware of the path or lacking the courage and conviction to choose it. The story must be told, told, and re-told. Positive change for all students must continue.

Look to the end of this book. There you will find a CD-ROM with Jim Hansen, Phil DiFrancesco, Gerv leyden and Gary Bunch in conversations about inclusion in education. In addition, there is a pictorial up-date of HWCDSB in celebration of its 30th year of inclusion (student produced). Students, teachers, parents, and administrators tell what inclusive experience has meant in their lives. There are also short articles by Jim, thoughts and musings as he continues his work.

Parents in our schools are given a simple promise.

To this day, we have kept that promise.

*Your child, able or disabled, is Welcome
and will be a full participant
in his or her school and class.*

Your child will never be removed permanently.

*In the event of any short-term removal,
for whatever reason, due process will be followed.*

And your child remains welcome to return.

Always.

Meet the Cast (Authors)

This book and DVD are the story of the origins of Inclusion. Jim Hansen and Phil DiFrancesco lived that history for decades. Jim compiled an historical record, and it took a whole team, led by Gerv Leyden and Gary Bunch from the universities of Nottingham and York respectively, allying with Jack Pearpoint (Inclusion Press) and Jeff Dobbin (Parashoot Productions) to create the book and DVD you see. In the DVD, Jim and Phil tell their stories, supplemented by Gerv's international perspective, and Gary's historical contextual frame.

Jim Hansen

James A. Hansen: (Jim) was born in Montreal. He began his career as an educator in 1952 in Toronto. He served as Teacher, Principal and Superintendent of Operations with the Hamilton Catholic School Board (HWCDSB) from 1959 until his retirement in 1991. In retirement he continues to advocate for inclusive schools where "Each Belongs".

Gerv Leyden

Gervase Leyden: is an educational psychologist with Local Education Authority (LEA) services in the United Kingdom. At the University of Nottingham, he trains educational psychologists (EP) and contributes to the EP doctoral programme. Gerv is also a Board Member of the Marsha Forest Centre, Toronto. His research interests focus on the education of vulnerable children and the application of educational, organizational and occupational psychology to school systems in order to build safer, healthier, inclusive learning environments for both children and staff.

Gary Bunch

Gary Bunch: is Chair of the Marsha Forest Centre, an advocate for inclusion, an author, a researcher, and a consultant on inclusion. He has been a teacher of deaf students, a residential school administrator, and a professor of education, psychology, and critical disability studies. Gary has authored many books including: Inclusion: How To; Inclusion: Recent Research; PlayFair Teams; and Crucial Terms. His commitment to inclusion has resulted in extensive work in India, as well as Ecuador, Qatar, Slovenia and Russia.

Jack Pearpoint

Jack Pearpoint: is the founding Director of Inclusion Press and the Marsha Forest Centre: Inclusion.Family.Community. He is an independent Canadian publisher and catalyst for Inclusion, Diversity, Teamwork and Change! Jointly with John O'Brien and Marsha Forest (deceased), Jack was part of the creation of planning tools such as Circles, MAPS and PATH, Tools for Change . Now, with his wife Lynda Kahn, Jack and John O'Brien conduct training events, workshops and 'institutes' around the world to assist organizations to deal with change, and build full lives for people with disabilities.

Phil DiFrancesco

Phil DiFrancesco: retired in 2001 as a Supervisory Officer with the HWCDSB after 35 years of service. Most of his career and community involvement focused on the inclusion of all students in their neighbourhood schools. He is an international speaker and served with the Ontario Ministry of Education to develop the Provincial inclusion policy. In retirement he continues to support parents of children with special needs.

INCLUSION PRESS ORDER FORM
24 Thome Crescent, Toronto, ON Canada M6H 2S5
Tel: 416-658-5363 Fax: 416-658-5067
E-mail: inclusionpress@inclusion.com WEB: http://www.inclusion.com

Inclusion SPECIAL PACKS... [** = new products]

All Means All PACK $110 + $10 shipping/pack ____
- Video: All Means All, plus book: All My Life's a Circle

The Community PACK $ 40 + $7 shipping/pack ____
- Members of Each Other & Celebrating the Ordinary - 2 books - John O'Brien & Connie Lyle O'Brien

The Education Book PACK $ 40 + $7 shipping/pack ____
- Inclusion: Recent Research & Inclusion: How To - 2 Books - Gary Bunch

Friendship PACK (1 book + Video) $ 60 + $10 shipping/pack ____
- [Friendship Video + From Behind the Piano/What's Really Worth Doing]

Inclusion Classics Book PACK [Action for Inclusion + Inclusion Papers] $ 30 + $7 shipping/pack ____

Inclusion Classics Videos PACK (DVD format also available) $ 90 + $12 shipping/pack ____
- Videos [With a Little Help from My Friends + Kids Belong Together]

PATH IN ACTION PACK (DVD format also available) $150 + $15 shipping/pack ____
- 2 Path Training Videos [(Path in Action + Path Training) + Path Workbook]

Petroglyphs PACK - Book & Video on Inclusion in High Schools - from UNH $ 60 + $10 shipping/pack ____

**PlayFair Teams Kit - Teacher's book, Advocate's book , Intro CD, 2 posters $ 65 + $10 shipping/pack ____

When Spider Webs Unite PACK - Shafik Asante - Book and Video $ 80 + $10 shipping/pack ____

Books

		Copies	Total
Action for Inclusion - Classic on Inclusion	$20 + $5 /1st copy shipping	____	____
All My Life's a Circle Expanded Edition- Circles, MAPS & PATH	$20 + $5 /1st copy shipping	____	____
The All Star Company - Team Building by Nick Marsh	$20 + $5 /1st copy shipping	____	____
The Careless Society - John McKnight	$25 + $5 /1st copy shipping	____	____
Celebrating the Ordinary O'Brien, O'Brien & Jacob	$25 + $5 /1st copy shipping	____	____
Circle of Friends by Bob & Martha Perske	$25 + $5 /1st copy shipping	____	____
Community Lost & Found Arthur Lockhart & Michael Clarke	$30 + $5 /1st copy shipping	____	____
Creating Circles of Friends - Colin Newton & Derek Wilson	$25 + $5 /1st copy shipping	____	____
Do You Hear What I Hear? - Janice Fialka & Karen Mikus	$15 + $5 /1st copy shipping	____	____
Dream Catchers & Dolphins Marsha Forest and Jack Pearpoint	$20 + $5 /1st copy shipping	____	____
**Each Belongs -Jim Hansen with Leyden, Bunch, Pearpoint (book with CD)	$30 + $5 /1st copy shipping	____	____
From Behind the Piano, by Jack Pearpoint AND **What's Really Worth Doing** by Judith Snow - Now in ONE Book *	$20 + $5 /1st copy shipping	____	____
Hints for Graphic Facilitators by Jack Pearpoint	$25 + $5 /1st copy shipping	____	____
Implementing Person-Centered Planning: Voices of Experience Edited by John O'Brien & Connie Lyle O'Brien	$25 + $5 /1st copy shipping	____	____
The Inclusion Papers - Strategies & Stories	$20 + $5 /1st copy shipping	____	____
Inclusion: How To Essential Classroom Strategies - Gary Bunch	$25+ $5 /1st copy shipping	____	____
Inclusion: Recent Research G. Bunch & A. Valeo	$25 + $5 /1st copy shipping	____	____
It Matters - Lessons from my Son - Janice Fialka	$15 + $5 /1st copy shipping	____	____
Kids, Disabilities Regular Classrooms Gary Bunch	$20 + $5 /1st copy shipping	____	____
Lessons for Inclusion Curriculum Ideas for Inclusion in Elementary Schools	$20 + $5 /1st copy shipping	____	____
A Little Book About Person Centered Planning Forest, Lovett, Mount, Pearpoint, Smull, Snow, and Strully	$20 + $5 /1st copy shipping	____	____
**Make a Difference: Direct Support Guidebook (J. O'Brien & B. Mount)	$20 + $5 shipping /1st copy	____	____
**Make a Difference: Leader's Resource Kit (Instructor's book + CD)	$30 + $5 shipping /1st copy	____	____
**Make a Difference: Learning Journey Booklet (packet of 10)	$20 + $5 shipping /1st set	____	____
Members of Each Other John O'Brien & Connie Lyle O'Brien	$25 + $5 /1st copy shipping	____	____
One Candle Power by Cathy Ludlum & Communitas	$25 + $5 /1st copy shipping	____	____
Path Workbook - 2nd Edition Planning Positive Possible Futures	$20 + $5 /1st copy shipping	____	____
Perske - Pencil Portraits 1971-1990	$30 + $5 /1st copy shipping	____	____
Person-Centred Planning with MAPS & PATH by John O'Brien & Jack Pearpoint	$25 + $5 /1st copy shipping	____	____
Petroglyphs - Inclusion in High School from UNH	$20 + $5 /1st copy shipping	____	____

**PlayFair Teams: A Manual for Teacher Advisors	$15 + $5 /1st copy shipping	____	
**PlayFair Teams: A Community Advocate's Manual	$15 + $5 /1st copy shipping	____	
Reflections on Inclusive Education	$15 + $5 /1st copy shipping	____	
Restorative Justice Art Lockhart, Lynn Zammit, Randy Charboneau	$30 + $5 /1st copy shipping	____	
**Supporting Learners with Intellectual Challenge Gary Bunch	$20 + $5 /1st copy shipping	____	
Treasures - from UNH	$20 + $5 /1st copy shipping	____	
Waddie Welcome & the Beloved Community T.Kohler & S.Earl	$25 + $5 /1st copy shipping	____	
When Spider Webs Unite Community & Inclusion- Shafik Asante	$20 + $5 /1st copy shipping	____	
Yes! She Knows She's Here Nicola Schaefer's Book about Kathrine	$20 + $5 /1st copy shipping	____	

Inclusion – Exclusion Poster (18 X 24)	$10 + $5 /1st copy shipping	____	
Person Centered Direct Support Foldout (call for bulk rates)	$ 5 + $2 /1st copy shipping	____	
Inclusion News in Bulk (box of 100)	$50 – includes shipping in NA	____	

MEDIA: VIDEOs • CD-ROMs • DVDs

All Means All - Inclusion Video Introduction to Circles, MAPS and PATH	$100 + $8 shipping /1st copy	____	
Dream Catchers (Dreams & Circles)	$55 + $8 shipping /1st copy	____	
Each Belongs (30 years of Inclusion-15 min. celebration in Hamilton)	$50 + $8 shipping /1st copy	____	
EVERYONE Has a GIFT John McKnight - Building Communities of Capacity	$75 + $8 shipping /1st copy	____	
**Finding Meaning in the Work - (CD + Manual) (O'Briens)	$195 + $8 shipping /1st copy	____	
Friendship Video Judith, Marsha & Jack on Friendship	$55 + $8 shipping /1st copy	____	
The Inclusion Classics - DVD (2 classic inclusion videos on DVD)	$ 90 + $8 shipping /1st copy	____	
Kids Belong Together - MAPS & Circles	$55 + $8 shipping /1st copy	____	
The MAPS Collection - DVD (2 MAPS Training videos on DVD)	$150 + $8 shipping /1st copy	____	
Miller's MAP - MAPS in Action	$55 + $8 shipping /1st copy	____	
**My Life, My Choice - DVD (7 stories of adults with full lives)	$150 + $8 shipping /1st copy	____	
NEW MAPS TRAINING Video Shafik's MAP - MAPS Process - Step by Step	$75 + $8 shipping /1st copy	____	
The PATH Collection - DVD (2 PATH Training videos on DVD)	$150 + $8 shipping /1st copy	____	
PATH Demo Video Univ of Dayton Ohio - Video of Workshop on PATH	$55 + $8 shipping /1st copy	____	
PATH IN ACTION Working with Groups -Training Video for Path with Groups	$100 + $8 shipping /1st copy	____	
PATH TRAINING Video Intro Training Video - An Individual Path (Joe's Path)	$75 + $8 shipping /1st copy	____	
Person Centered Direct Support - CD - 4 minute video & powerpoint	$ 25 + $8 shipping /1st copy	____	
Petroglyphs Video Companion to Petroglyphs Book - **Packaged with book**	$60 + $8 shipping /1st copy	____	
**PlayFair Teams DVD an introduction to PlayFair Teams -	$50 + $8 shipping /1st copy	____	
ReDiscovering MAPS Charting Your Journey -brand NEW MAPS training video	$100 + $8 shipping /1st copy	____	
Together We're Better (3 videos) Staff Development Kit	$175 + $12 shipping	____	

TOOLS FOR CHANGE - The CD-Rom for Person Centred Planning
Pricing is dependent on a licensing agreement. To obtain licensing information check our website, e-mail or call us.

When Spider Webs Unite - Video Shafik Asante in Action	$75 + $8 /1st copy shipping	____	
With a Little Help from My Friends The Classic on Circles & MAPS	$55 + $8 /1st copy shipping	____	

Plus applicable taxes (variable)

GRAND TOTAL $===========

Tools for Change

CD - Tools for Person Centered Planning

New Resources:
- **My Life My Choice** - DVD - Seven Adults living full lives
- **Make a Difference** - book; training pack, note kit
- **Each Belongs** - book & CD - The 1st Inclusive School Board ever!
- **PlayFair Teams** - 2 books, DVD + Posters - blended teams in schools.
- **Find Meaning in the Work** - CD & Manual - presentation ready!
- **Supporting Learners with Intellectual Challenge** -teacher resources

Name: _____
Organization:_____
Address:_____
City: _____
Prov/State _____ Post Code/ZIP _____
Wk Phone _____ Cheque Enclosed _____
Hm Phone _____ Fax _____
E-Mail _____ Web Page:_____

April, 2006 Listing